PENGUIN
SUPER 30

Dr Biju Mathew, FRCPC, is a consultant psychiatrist and a clinical associate professor at the University of British Columbia. After completing a medical degree in India, he obtained his postgraduate training in the United Kingdom before settling down in Canada to pursue his career.

He is a teacher and researcher, and has been involved in the care of the mentally ill through his professional career. He is an avid advocate for the underprivileged and those marginalized in society, including the homeless and the stigmatized. His activism and work in multiculturalism is well recognized. He continues to provide leadership roles for his profession and works tirelessly for charitable causes. His work resonates well with the work of Anand Kumar of Super 30, which led to Dr Mathew's authorship of Anand's biography.

Dr Mathew resides with his wife, Grace, in Maple Ridge, a beautiful suburb of Vancouver. He wishes to thank the members of his family, including his sons, Nick and Richie, and their spouses, Preetpal and Charmaine, sister, Jolly, and her husband, Vijay, for their support; and his grandson, Emery, who provides him with unlimited happiness. He enjoys playing squash and expresses himself through oil paintings.

ADVANCE PRAISE FOR *SUPER 30*

'Education is the only ladder to climb out of the clutches of poverty and exploitation. Anand Kumar's Super 30 students are great inspiration for the youth of today. They're an ingenious manifestation of what a passionate investment can yield.'

Kailash Satyarthi, Nobel Peace laureate;
and founder, Kailash Satyarthi Children's Foundation

'Handicapped by his own modest background, this brilliant mathematician Anand turned his failure to gain higher education into an inspirational success story by making sure that hundreds of students from impoverished and backward societies did not suffer the same fate! Super 30 empowers them to believe they CAN!'

Prakash Jha, film-maker and screenwriter

'I first met Anand Kumar in the summer of 2003. We were waiting for a bus together at a mathematics conference in Boulder, Colorado. He seemed out of place, but he approached me and asked, in poor English, if I would look at a set of problems which he had written. As I was off from teaching that summer, I eventually looked at the problem set. It was very good. I made some corrections— mainly to the English language usage and replied to the email address he had given me. This began a series of correspondences lasting several years. Anand is very clever and a master of problem-solving techniques and yet so modest and soft-spoken. These are keys to greatness; but without Anand's determination and virtuous goals, he would not have achieved his international acclaim. He serves as an inspiration and guide to all of his students—as he should to all of those who read this book.'

Peter L. Vachuska, PhD, emeritus professor of mathematics, University of Wisconsin–Washington County

'Good education is a gift that empowers, and Anand has been able to show hundreds of disadvantaged students a path to success and modern livelihood, thereby also lifting their families out of poverty. Anand's story is one that must be told as widely as possible, a story that is wholly Indian and wholly subaltern. By detailing the circumstances in which Anand came to do what he does, this book will inspire several other people to give back to the societies they grew up in . . . I had the pleasure of hosting Anand for a talk at Stanford University and I was touched by his simplicity and humility. I hold Anand in great reverence, and I wish him, his team and all his students the very best.'

PhD student in physics, Stanford University; IIT JEE 2006 All India Rank 1; and AIEEE 2006 All India Rank 1

SUPER 30

CHANGING THE WORLD 30 STUDENTS AT A TIME

ANAND KUMAR

BIJU MATHEW

PENGUIN BOOKS

PENGUIN BOOKS

Published by the Penguin Group

Penguin Books India Pvt. Ltd, 7th Floor, Infinity Tower C, DLF Cyber City, Gurgaon 122 002, Haryana, India

Penguin Group (USA) Inc., 375 Hudson Street, New York, New York 10014, USA

Penguin Group (Canada), 90 Eglinton Avenue East, Suite 700, Toronto, Ontario, M4P 2Y3, Canada

Penguin Books Ltd, 80 Strand, London WC2R 0RL, England

Penguin Ireland, 25 St Stephen's Green, Dublin 2, Ireland
(a division of Penguin Books Ltd)

Penguin Group (Australia), 707 Collins Street, Melbourne, Victoria 3008, Australia

Penguin Group (NZ), 67 Apollo Drive, Rosedale, Auckland 0632, New Zealand

Penguin Books (South Africa) (Pty) Ltd, Block D, Rosebank Office Park, 181 Jan Smuts Avenue, Parktown North, Johannesburg 2193, South Africa

Penguin Books Ltd, Registered Offices: 80 Strand, London WC2R 0RL, England

First published by Penguin Books India 2016

ISBN 9780143426448

For sale in the Indian Subcontinent only

Typeset in Palatino by Manipal Digital Systems, Manipal
Printed at Thomson Press India Ltd, New Delhi

A PENGUIN RANDOM HOUSE COMPANY

Special thanks to
Robert Prince,
Radhika Marwah
and Arun Kumar

Contents

Prologue

30 May 2008 dawned bright and clear in Patna, Bihar. Pans were rattling and children were being coaxed out of beds and into school uniforms. It was early still, but the slum of Chandpur Bela was abuzz. People were gravitating towards one house—Shanti Kutir. A crowd was assembled and if you pushed in farther, you could see a youngish man in his shirtsleeves, who seemed the centre of all the hullaballoo.

Anand Kumar was trying to talk to several people at once, answering questions, accepting their good wishes, and trying his utmost not to let his anxiety and nerves show. He had spent the previous year coaching thirty students for the IIT JEE entrance examination and finally, it was the day of the results. It was the hour of reckoning. All thirty students had spent the night at Anand's house, all too keyed up to get any sleep. Anand relived this year after year, yet the tight bundle of nerves in his stomach would not ease till he saw each student's result. By 6 a.m., they had given up all pretence of sleep and started to get dressed. Jayanti Devi, Anand's mother, prepared tea and soon the modest Kumar household was bustling with people.

Journalists started arriving as early as 6.30 a.m. Anand tried to explain to the first few that the results would not be out until 9 a.m., but soon gave up when he saw that they also wanted to capture the mood before the results were announced.

By 2008, Super 30 was a name to reckon with. Anand Kumar was hailed as a hero by *People* magazine, and his unique initiative, Super 30, was celebrated as one of the four most innovative schools in the world by *Newsweek* magazine. Expectations were sky high as twenty-eight students had cracked the coveted IIT entrance exam the previous year, in 2007. Anand fielded calls from journalists who had grown close to him over the past few years as Super 30's fame spread. *I hope the result doesn't disappoint*, prayed Anand, as 9 a.m. ticked nearer. Outwardly, he was the picture of calm—reassuring the students, charming the media.

At about quarter to nine, Anand positioned himself in front of the computer screen with a list of roll numbers in hand. The students huddled around and more and more people pressed themselves into the cramped room. At 9.01 a.m., Rakesh Kumar was in! A cheer went up, Rakesh was thumped on the back, a journalist surreptitiously tried to lead him outside so he could get an interview. Anand Kumar still had twenty-nine more names to go. Everybody waited with bated breath as he keyed in the second roll number. But nothing happened. The server was jammed. Lakhs of aspirants were simultaneously trying to check their scores. A few minutes later, Jai Ram had made it through! And now it was eighteen on eighteen. Anand was perspiring freely but a hint of a smile played on his lips. He went on checking result after result—sometimes it would pop up immediately leading to raucous cheers and in other moments the error page would come up. Nearly an hour and a half later, it was just Anand and Ranjan Kumar, the thirtieth student left at the computer. *'Chinta mat kariye, sab achha hoga,'* Anand said to the white-faced Ranjan. He had made it. He hugged Anand tightly and started laughing, and then crying, and then shouting garbled victory cries.

Anand was hoisted on shoulders, laddus were thrust into his mouth, flashbulbs went off, headlines for next morning's papers were composed, and cries of *'Anand sir zindabad'* reverberated. Deepu Kumar's father had travelled from Supaul to be with them for the occasion. He was so overcome with emotion that he stood alone in a corner, weeping. Anand Sahay's mother sat with Jayanti Devi making puris and jalebis. Journalists were trying to talk to as many students as they could. It was surreal. Anand could hardly believe it. Looking down at the shining, jubilant faces of his students, he felt a happiness so piercing that tears pricked his eyes.

History had been made. Super 30 had achieved a cent per cent result.

1

A Hero's Welcome

30 September 2014—MIT Media Lab

Anand Kumar stood on stage in an ordinary shirt and worn pair of pants. He was fidgety, but confident, a small smile played about his lips—a smile which conveyed awe and disbelief. He felt a strange sense of unreality. He was standing in front of the most august gathering he could imagine—professors and students of the Massachusetts Institute of Technology in Boston, readying to deliver a talk on his unique school, Super 30. *Strange, the ways of this world,* thought Anand. *Not so long ago I was taking rounds down galis on my cycle selling papads in the neighbourhood, trying hard to forget my shattered dream of studying at Cambridge, and here I am today.*

He shook his head and began: 'Thank you for giving me this platform and opportunity to speak before you today. It's hard to believe that I have been invited to speak at one of the world's top institutions. This very institution, MIT, is the dream destination for many to pursue higher education and today I have the opportunity to be here.

'I have come from Bihar, a state in India that was once known for its glorious traditions in the field of education with institutions like Nalanda University and Vikramshila. But today it is at the bottom of the ladder on virtually all parameters of the human index. Around 40 per cent of the population cannot read and write, which itself points to the pitiable situation in Bihar.

'I am not here to tell you anything new. All I want to say is that education remains the most powerful weapon to tackle most of the world's problems today, as most of the problems have their genesis in poverty and ignorance. Super 30 is a step towards eradicating this and I begin with hope; hope that no matter how violent the storm, the ship can emerge unscathed with the grit and guidance of a deft hand.

'Picture this boy: Santosh, from a cripplingly poor family living in a village 40 kilometres from Patna, the capital of Bihar. He lived near the highway with his father and mother, and the family made a living selling vegetables. Santosh went to a school where teachers never turned up and spent his evening helping his father at the vegetable thela.

'Santosh understood the power of education. So did his parents. He studied till Class X but didn't know how to continue after that. He was good at mathematics so everybody around him told him to study for IIT, so he decided to go to Patna. He realized that coaching in Patna was very expensive and there was no way he could afford it. It was here that he found out about Super 30, gave the entrance test and got chosen for the programme. He got through IIT Kharagpur. Santosh's journey from a roadside vendor to a research scholar in Europe got a lot of media attention in Japan, Germany and the US apart from India. There was even a documentary made about how from studying by a lantern, with no electricity, and at times no food, he had scaled such heights. Today he is in Europe at a well-known university.

'Now let me tell you about Anup. Anup lived in Chenw, a remote village of Bihar which was riddled with Naxalite trouble. Anup's family struggled to feed themselves. One night, eight-year-old Anup was crying due to hunger. His mother beseeched his father to go out and ask someone for some rice so they could boil it and eat it with salt. But the water boiled and boiled till there was nothing left in the pan. Anup's father never returned. Some say he got captured by the Naxals; the villagers looked for him for many days but there was no trace of him. Anup grew up—first sad and then angry at the abject poverty he was surrounded by. He grew disenchanted by the vast divide between the poor and rich in the country. He was lured by the methods of the Naxals and looked for ways to exact revenge, but his mother knew there was only one weapon powerful enough—education. She toiled hard and sent Anup to school. He scored very well in his Class X exams and came to Patna to get advice on higher education. They landed up at the Janata Darbaar in Patna at Nitish Kumar's house. Their story was received with sympathy but it was clear that they could not offer any direct support. However, seeing the young boy's helplessness, someone at the chief minister's house suggested that they go meet Anand Kumar, as they were told he coached some students without taking a penny from them.

'When I first set eyes on Anup and his mother, they were barefoot and glistening in sweat but there was a light in their eyes. Anup studied hard for two years, and is in his third year at IIT Bombay today.'

After every story and with the accompanying images on the screen behind Anand, the audience would gasp, some breaking into applause without realizing that they were clapping in the middle of a presentation.

Anand went on to tell them about some more students like Santosh and Anup. He told them about Anupam whose father was an autorickshaw driver, and many others like him who could climb out of the hellhole of poverty by catching onto the lifeline Super 30 extended.

'Now I would like to tell you about Super 30. Super 30 is a programme for underprivileged students, which I started back in 2002. I have also seen poverty very closely. I know the pain of destitution. My father was a lowly clerk in the postal department of India. I wanted to be a mathematician and was always busy trying to arrive at new results in mathematics. I had written some mathematical papers in my college life and these papers were published in reputed foreign journals. I got an opportunity to study at the University of Cambridge for higher education in mathematics, but due to lack of funds I could not make it there. I tried very hard to get some help, but at the time all doors were slammed shut in my face. My world was already shattered when on top of my dejection, I suddenly lost my father. The responsibility of feeding the family and managing our dismal affairs rested on my shoulders. At that time my younger brother was a disciple of Padma Bhushan N. Rajam and was learning to play the violin under her tutelage in Banaras Hindu University. I got an offer for a job in the postal department on compassionate grounds after the demise of my father, but I refused the offer and started to teach mathematics to willing students of the neighbourhood. I rented a small room nearby and the students would pay me whatever they could afford. But we needed money to survive. My mother made papad, a savoury Indian snack, and I would go door to door on my cycle selling these. It was humiliating at times but I never lost hope and courage. Gradually, the rush of students increased and my programme became famous among the underprivileged students of Bihar state. Once, a very bright student came to me and indicated that he had no capacity to pay even 500 rupees for a year as my fee. But he assured me that he would pay the amount when his father harvested potatoes from his farm. I asked him how he would live in Patna to attend my classes. He replied that he would camp out under the stairs at the house of a rich man.

'I'll admit I was a little sceptical and decided to pay this boy a surprise visit. The sight of this boy, eyes scrunched up in concentration, studying a physics book, shook me. It reminded me of my days of hardship. This event became the source of inspiration to start the programme, Super 30. I called my brother Pranav Kumar, by now a talented violinist working in Mumbai, and we put our heads together to start the Super 30 programme. Pranav used to help me earlier as well, but now he was directly involved and entrusted with the responsibility of managing Super 30. After thorough screening, thirty poor but talented students, from underprivileged sections, were shortlisted to be part of Super 30. The idea was to impart IIT coaching completely free of charge, including boarding and meals. Initially, making arrangements for thirty students was not so easy, but my family extended all the help they could in this endeavour. I generated finance by tutoring students who could pay, while my mother, Jayanti Devi, cooked for the students. For the students, there was only one goal—to study hard and not be distracted by other problems. After the initial success, I received a lot of offers of monetary donations but I refused politely. Many people ask me the reason why I don't accept financial help. The reason is very clear: I want to prove that even in Bihar, the most backward state of India, if you have the desire and determination, you can do anything you wish. Lack of resources and infrastructure need not hold anyone back.

'When my programme started running successfully, I got appreciation, but at the same time the coaching mafia of Patna rallied forces against me. Coaching is a very lucrative industry in Patna, and the success and growing popularity of Super 30 loomed as a threat to them. Thrice I was attacked by armed criminals. Once, one of my non-teaching staff members, Munna, was injured very badly. A knife was thrust in his stomach and he struggled for his life for three months in a hospital. Some of my friends asked me why I was running Super 30 despite such risks. But I never lost courage. The government provided me with two armed bodyguards and they are still with me. When results started coming in, we were overjoyed and a little amazed. The very first year, eighteen students made it. The second year twenty-two students, the third year twenty-six students, the fourth year twenty-eight students, the fifth year twenty-eight, and for three consecutive years all thirty students out of thirty cleared the entrance test for IIT. The students who didn't make it to IIT got into various other prestigious engineering colleges. In the last twelve years, 308 students qualified for the IIT JEE. Now, the mafia leaves me alone but they resort to other tactics. Recently, there has been a mushrooming of Super 30s prefixed by names like Gaya, Nalanda, even Raja, Baja. On the signboard, they write Mumbai, Raja or Baja in tiny font size and Super 30 in bold. The objective is to cash in on Super 30's success by taking innocent students for a ride. Their objective is to mint money from this programme and take donations from the government as well as from the private sector. Sometimes, it makes things problematic for me too. But mostly people can filter out the truth from these imitators.

'Another question that I frequently encounter wherever I go is: "Anand, what is the secret behind the success of Super 30?"

'Well, there is no magic, nor am I any different from other human beings. I am a very simple teacher. Success never comes easy. I feel that during the training of underprivileged students, the most important thing is to raise their level of confidence. Having lived in deprivation for so long, they lose all their aspirations despite being as talented as any other child next door.

'But then, doing this is not so easy. It is really a difficult task, as the students from poor families invariably start off with a crippling inferiority complex. For us, the first objective is to pull them out of the cloud of despondency and make them believe in their own abilities. Once they are mentally prepared to study for the IIT JEE, half the battle is won, for confidence makes them more focused. They also start feeling that they are as good as any other student from the well-to-do families.

'To constantly reinforce this point, I created two characters—Bholu and Ricky. While Ricky is from a privileged family, Bholu comes from a poor family. Ricky wears branded clothes, but Bholu wears a simple kurta pyjama. Ricky eats pizza and burgers, while Bholu eats simple Indian food like corn and chapattis. Ricky rides a motorbike, while Bholu rides an old bicycle. Ricky speaks in English, while Bholu speaks in the local tongue. The first part of my example always suggests the contrasting lifestyles of the privileged and the not-so-privileged. But the second part is about how lifestyle doesn't make any difference to what they achieve. When a mathematical problem is presented to both of them, Ricky provides only one solution, which he was taught by his teacher. He does it exactly in textbook style and quickly, while Bholu struggles with it. But ultimately, Bholu explores new ways and solves the problem through various methods.

'There are two advantages of doing this. My students also get to learn that for success, there is always a level playing field, irrespective of who is born where. So, Bholu becomes the role model for my students. Bholu teaches them never to give up, as success is the only way they can turn the tide in their favour. With hard work as their main strength, they don't take long to achieve that. In the examination hall, they tend to tackle even tricky questions with full confidence.

'Now I want to see every underprivileged student educated. Now I have a dream. I want to see my students at MIT. It is my great dream. Some of my students have got the chance to study in good American universities and are working here. But no one has managed to get into MIT so far. I don't know if my dream will be fulfilled or not. But I know that I have to continue to labour hard for my goal. Presently, I am teaching at a makeshift school under a tin shed in the hope that my students will be here. I want to see my students as Nobel prize winners, Field prize winners.

'I have not come here to ask for anything. As you know, I don't accept any financial help. I have come all this distance to appeal to all you great technology experts that technology should not just remain a tool to make big money. It should be made a vital weapon in the fight against illiteracy so that even the poorest have access to quality education. Today, I feel technology has emerged as a big tool to make huge profits and reduce dependence on manual work. But now the time has come to think about how it could be used to fight poverty, which affects people the world over. The time has come to move out of the labs to get a first-hand feel of poverty in nations and villages, where people don't even get basic electricity and clean water. That will add a human dimension to technology that the world needs to make it a better place. War machines can win us wars, but they cannot bring us peace and enlightenment.

'Today, the world wants technology to save humanity and give it dignity. And it requires cooperation from all sections. A beautiful world is what we all need—a world free from poverty and illiteracy, a world with true understanding and compassion.'

With that, Anand Kumar ended. He stood on stage, eyes shining with tears, a wide smile on his face. He raised both his hands, bowed, looked abashed, but the thundering applause didn't peter down. People were standing and clapping, a fair few teary-eyed. They had seen a display of unabashed honesty and raw grit. They had seen a man's struggle against his destiny and his selflessness. And this man asked nothing of them. This was goosebumps-inducing stuff.

He got down from the stage, head still bowed, quite overwhelmed with the response. *White people are standing and clapping for me. Some people are also crying,* he thought, amazed, looking around him. People approached him for photos and to talk to him. He obliged everybody and tried to respond to the questions as well as he could.

In the car, on his way back from MIT Media Labs, Anand sat in the back looking at trees whizzing past, the orderly traffic, the clear blue sky, and saw limitless opportunity. He looked to his side and smiled at his brother

Pranav who was sitting beside him. 'How far we have come, bhaiya,' Pranav said. 'How proud pitaji would have been today!'

'Yes, he always saw something in me which I myself could not. I still remember the times he would joke with me and compete to touch my feet when I tried to touch his. How we would joke! He embarrassed me and always said, "What if I'm not around when you become a big man? Let me pay my respects when I can."' Anand shook his head and couldn't hold the tears back.

Pranav put his arm around his elder brother's shoulders, valiantly trying to hold his emotions in check. 'Pitaji is up there somewhere, watching us, bhaiya. It's only because of all his blessings that you were addressing an audience at MIT earlier today.'

Anand smiled ruefully and thought back to the time when his world seemed to be shrinking and he was beset by one setback after another. He hadn't accepted his fate then, and he continued to dream even today.

'Yes, he is. Super 30 is a very small initiative in the grand scheme of things and I want to make this bigger so I can realize the dream Pitaji nurtured from the beginning. I want to help more students and multiply the effect we have seen with Super 30.'

There are some people who don't let their circumstances hold them back. Anand Kumar was one of them. Like Oscar Wilde said, 'We are all in the gutter, but some of us are looking at the stars.'

StudentSpeak

Name: Shashi Narayan

Super 30 Batch: 2004

Institute and Stream: Computer Science and Engineering, IIT Kharagpur

Current Job: Research Associate, University of Edinburgh

Looking back at my career, becoming a part of Super 30 was the life-turning event for me. I remember when I first moved to Patna for JEE preparation and within a couple of months I realized the horror of being lost in the crowd. Being from a less privileged family, I am very thankful to my parents who never set a limit for me. With their encouragement I got selected for Super 30 and the rest of what happened was all because of Super 30.

I think in Patna and many other places, many students, especially students from poor economic backgrounds, have potential but lack proper guidance. Super 30 is a heaven for such bright students. It provided us with a perfect environment for study, rigorous and caring guardianship, and of course great friends—and all these free of cost. It pulled out the fear in us of being lost in the crowd and pushed us to a level where we started to believe that even with our background, we can succeed. For me, that feeling and inner strength was very special and all that came because of Anand sir and Super 30. I feel lucky for being part of such a great institution and not being a product of the Kota factory.

After Super 30, I went on to do my major in Computer Science and Engineering from IIT Kharagpur. Anand sir always used to say I should go for higher studies. I believe that it was with his blessings that I continued with my higher studies. Currently, I am a research associate at the University of Edinburgh, one of the leading universities in the world.

I feel proud with the success stories of Super 30 in the following years. I hope that in the near future we will work more on such institutions, which provide guidance to students from lower backgrounds about different career prospects.

2

A Messiah Is Born

Rajendra Prasad lived in Gaudiya Math, a slum in the small district of Mitapur, a suburb of Patna, with his wife, Jayanti, his parents and his invalid brother. He worked as a letter sorter in the railway mail service, and made just enough to keep the wolf from the door. Starvation was never far away, but the family eked out just enough to afford food and the rent on a home that was modest even by Patna standards. Two eight-foot by eight-foot bedrooms, a shared kitchen and verandah accommodated two households—Rajendra and Jayanti occupied one half, while his brother Meena and his family occupied the other half. Their parents had no room to themselves and would sometimes sleep in Rajendra's room and other times in Meena's.

The Prasads were among the seventy-five million people that populated Bihar in 1973, of whom 70 per cent were living below the Indian poverty line, compared with about 54 per cent nationally. Indian GDP growth was less than 1 per cent nationwide, and Bihar was not a significant beneficiary of even this modest increase.

Poverty is a constricting affliction; the well-to-do cannot imagine how the poor carry on day after day, living in the conditions they do. But poor people find joy too. There are things which can raise you out of the blackest despair, and one such joy knocked on the Prasads' door, and it couldn't have arrived at a better time.

1 January 1973 was a cold winter's evening and Rajendra Prasad was away

on work to Calcutta. In Gaudiya Math, his wife Jayanti Devi was perspiring heavily and was in great convulsions of pain. Her water had just broken and the women had taken her into a separate room. Shanti Devi determinedly instructed the two other women and reassured Jayanti in soothing tones. But in her heart, she was afraid.

The family had been in a pall of gloom ever since Rajendra Prasad's youngest brother Narendra had succumbed to cancer five years earlier. He had been only eighteen years old. The family had had high hopes for Narendra because he was a bright young man who had in him the makings of a doctor, but unfortunately fate had its own agenda. Instead of rescuing the family from their poverty by becoming a doctor, Narendra and his cancer cost them every last rupee they had in the effort to save his life. They spent a whole year at the Tata Cancer Centre in Bombay, but in the end the cancer triumphed.

The agony of this loss took a toll on the whole family, but it was hardest on Shanti Devi. She was devastated by the loss. Days passed, but the grief didn't. The family was afraid that she was depressed and thought maybe a change in scenery might help her. She decided to visit with some relatives in Delhi and stay with them for a while. Things got worse when Rajendra Prasad and Jayanti Devi lost their six-month-old daughter to a brief illness. These relatives were in dire straits too but they were kind enough to offer some respite to Shanti Devi from the house of horrors which Gaudiya Math had become for her.

In Delhi, desperate to find some peace, Shanti Devi went to a dana-wallah baba, someone who would hear out your ills and then give you a few grains to cure you. She was inconsolable when she told the baba about her young son and granddaughter who had died suddenly. The baba gave her a grain and told her, 'Why do you cry and clutch at your hair? Your son is well and on his way. Go back to your home.' Shanti Devi was astounded but had faith. She took a train back to Patna that same night and arrived to find Jayanti Devi pregnant with a child. She clutched her daughter-in-law to her and whispered: 'Don't worry. Our ill fortune will pass.'

The pregnancy was very delicate since Jayanti Devi had lost a child just a few months before and was in very fragile physical and mental health. It was this second tragedy which had propelled the family deeper into despair. So it was to hope and promise that Shanti Devi returned from Delhi and from then on she took it upon herself to take great care of her daughter-in-law.

✎

Their house was situated at a distance of fifteen feet from the railway tracks and every time a train passed by, the cramped house rattled and the ground beneath shook. On 1 January, with the women locked in one room, each member of the family dealt with their personal demons and prayed fervently for some good news.

When Shanti Devi held the child in her hands, she smiled a real smile after years. *'Mera beta waapis aa gaya,'* she kept repeating like a mantra. Rajendra's father, Kamta Prasad, who was pacing in the street while his son Meena sat quietly on the verandah, heard the squeals emanating from the house and rushed inside. It seemed a miracle. Their family had suffered such misfortune recently that they had started to believe that nothing besides this depressing existence was their lot in life.

Shanti Devi brought the child swathed in a coarse blanket to the two men. Meena was overjoyed and felt a pang that his brother was not there at that moment. Moreover, he was greatly relieved to see his mother smile again. Suddenly the house, which had seemed ghostly and shadowed, burbled with happiness and hope. They hugged each other and cried with joy. Neighbours hearing the loud voices joined them soon outside and soon the entire neighbourhood knew that the Prasads had been blessed with a healthy baby boy.

Two days later, Rajendra Prasad alighted from the train, unaware of what awaited him at home. He was quite anxious and wanted to reach his wife quickly as he knew how nervous she was about this pregnancy. On the way, he came across Ramesh Sharma who teased him about becoming a father and congratulated him heartily. Rajendra was stunned. Because of lack of means of communication, he had no idea that the baby had been born. As he neared his house, he quickened his steps, and ran the remaining few metres. His brother, Meena, embraced him, shouting, *'Ladka hua hai'* and Rajendra sank to the ground on his knees, eyes heavenwards, hands clasped together in deliverance.

He saw his mother and wife, and Shanti Devi said with tears of joy, *'Anand aa gaya! Ab sab theek ho jaega.'*

Anand grew up in Gaudiya Math, which was sandwiched between a main road leading into Patna and the Delhi-Howrah railway line, the busiest in Bihar. The tracks were, and are, kept busy with carrying cargo and passengers from central India to the eastern part of the subcontinent. Anand, true to his name, brought happiness to the Prasad family and at times they forgot that they lived in squalor and inches away from debilitating poverty.

Anand's grandfather, Kamta, would carry the toddler on his shoulders when he went to the temple or attended other social functions. On rainy days, or in the scorching sun, he would take off his lungi and cover the boy's face to protect him from the inclement weather and walk to his house in just his checkered knickers.

Anand's grandfather played the tabla as a hobby, and the youngster enjoyed imitating the drumming actions by banging away on his toys, or even, when toys weren't at hand, by hitting imaginary drums with his fingers. Unfortunately, his grandfather passed away when Anand was just three years old, so he didn't have the benefit of his wisdom and love for very long. But the rest of the family made up for the loss by being even more attentive after Kamta Prasad's passing.

Two years after Anand's birth, the family grew again with the birth of his brother, Pranav, who became Anand's best friend. The three-foot by six-foot hallway in their home was their playground in those earliest years before school. Meena's son, Om Kumar, completed the trio of their immediate circle, but all of the children in the surrounding streets of Gaudiya Math were constant playmates for the three boys.

Anand was quite a mischievous, curious young boy. His mother would often find him getting into scraps of one kind or another, most of them of his own making.

He wanted to know how everything worked. He wanted to know why motor cars ran on petrol and not water, why torches and radios used batteries. While other kids were content playing with their toys, his joy chiefly came from taking a toy apart to see how it worked.

When Anand first came across a magnet, he was completely fascinated. He wanted to know why only certain pieces of iron were magnetic and why these attracted only metals and not non-metals. He asked many of his friends, but got varied answers. One of the elders he pestered told him that a piece of iron develops its magnetic quality after it was administered an electric shock. So Anand had to try it out for himself. He used some loose-hanging wires around his home and ended up causing a short circuit. There was a loud bang and the lights went out. Anand was shocked. Fearing punishment from his elders he ran and hid some way off. He only approached the house after the landlord repaired the fuse and the lights came back on.

Another friend told him that if iron was placed on a railway track and a train passed over it, it would develop magnetic qualities because of the pressure. Anand became excited and immediately took some scrap iron to the tracks behind his house. Friends in tow, Anand carefully placed the iron on the tracks and waited. Soon enough, a train came along and ran over the metal. A gleeful Anand examined it for signs of magnetism after the train had passed, but was disappointed. It wasn't until later in his schooling that he realized he had needed a magnetic field to magnetize his pieces of iron and not merely pressure or electricity.

However, despite the consequences, the experimentation was a key part of his early years.

As he grew up, family members and neighbours became used to Anand's particular ways and penchant for solving challenges. When he was ten or eleven, he made a game out of creating imaginary radios. Naturally, those imaginary radios required imaginary antennae, which had to be mounted as high up as possible in order to get the best reception. This led to many climbing incidents, not all of them successful. His cries after a tumble during one of these antenna expeditions up the nearest pole became common enough that people in the neighbourhood would shake their heads and say, 'It must be Anand.'

Eventually, he graduated from imaginary radios to real ones, and anytime he found a broken radio he would bring it home and try to repair it. In these efforts he completely ruined many of them, but the experiments weren't always disasters and a day finally came when he managed to repair a radio all by himself. It only worked for a short time, but it was a defining moment for young Anand because he had learned that with perseverance, you could overcome a challenge.

Music was an integral part of the Prasad family's traditions. Taking after his grandfather, Anand won first prize in a tabla competition at the famous Rabindra Bhavan Art Theatre in Patna, when he was just eleven years old. Meena played the harmonium, and remembers fondly how outstanding and engrossing Anand's performance was.

Rajendra Prasad was keen for Anand to go to a good school. He understood very well that education was the only way out of the clutches of poverty, and tried to drill it into Anand's head as well. When he was four years old, Anand was enrolled at St. Joseph's Convent School in Patna.

Always a perceptive child, Anand keenly observed the stark differences between the

better-off students and him. While tattered
clothes and no money to buy even roadside
goodies were common features in Gaudiya
Math, here the well-scrubbed, pampered
faces of other students rankled. But he did
not suffer long. Being a private institution, it
was difficult for Rajendra to afford his son's
education there, and when he was in Class IV,
Anand was transferred to Model St. Xavier's
School. This was the first time, though sadly
not the last, that Anand learned how money
was a privilege and how poverty closed
doors of opportunities in your face.

Rajendra Prasad would wake Anand up
early in the morning with chai and even sing
to him to get him out of bed. Anand would
jump out of bed and touch his father's feet.
At times, embarrassingly enough for Anand,
his father would touch his feet back, as if
competing with him. 'You might become a

big man some day, whose feet people touch. What if I'm not around then?' he'd counter laughing when Anand would protest. These morning chats were very significant to the shaping of this young man. Rajendra Prasad may have been poor, but he was intelligent and discussed things of import with Anand. Anand's politics and his world view were deeply shaped by his father's experiences and sensitivity.

Rajendra Prasad grew up in a village called Deodaha, just thirty kilometres from Patna, though it may well have been 1000 kilometres away, given how dissimilar the two places were. Patna was a big city, while Deodaha had a population of only 2000 back in the 1950s when Rajendra was a boy. The Prasad family owned several parcels of land jointly, and Rajendra's father, Kamta Prasad, was the patriarch. In Bihar, as in much of India at the time, land was everything, and the wealthiest families were great landowners who treated their workers little better than serfs. Kamta Prasad had land, but he was a small landowner and money was a rare commodity for the family, even though he was also the village doctor. He practised traditional medicine for grateful neighbours, but their ability to pay was minimal and so Kamta Prasad's children were lucky to have a shirt and one pair of shorts to last them a year.

Ironically, though he was the village doctor, eight of Kamta's children would die before reaching adulthood, such being the result of a deadly combination of poor sanitation, a lack of modern medicine and too little food. Knowing that education was likely to be the only way his son could ever rise above the life of misery that pervaded rural Bihar, Kamta encouraged Rajendra to pay attention to his books, and to get as much education as he could. Years later, Rajendra would do the same with Anand. This was much easier said than done, however, because for a child in Deodaha, getting an education was no easy task. The nearest school was almost eight kilometres away, and a young boy from the farms who wanted to go to school had to walk there and back daily to pursue his studies.

When he was young, Rajendra felt that his brother Meena, who had a limp since childhood, should also have an opportunity to study, and so he would carry his elder brother on his shoulders to school each day. Even on the most hot and humid days, he would do it, despite sweating profusely in the blistering heat and stopping many a times to catch his breath.

Rajendra was an excellent student and completed Class X with first-class marks. In 1961, he set out to pursue higher studies in Patna, and so moved to Gaudiya Math where he would be the first in his family to become a college graduate.

In 1966, Rajendra married Jayanti and together, with Meena, they moved into the cramped, two-bedroom accommodation that would eventually see the birth of Anand Kumar.

One day, a blast was heard throughout the neighbourhood of Chandpur Bela, shocking its residents out of their routine and out of their homes. The people present outside saw an enormous white light before it went dark, leaving only the plastic burning with a small fire. The orchestrator of this crime was none other than the inquisitive Anand Kumar, who was now eleven years of age.

'What happened?' Jayanti Devi asked, glaring at her son. His antics were now becoming part of their daily routine, but this one had been of a magnitude she had not conceived him to be capable of. The neighbours seemed extremely annoyed. The eleven-year-old boy glanced at his mother and the growing audience sheepishly, before quickly putting out the remaining fire with a bucket of dirt he had kept next to himself. Seeing this evidence of premeditation, Jayanti Devi found herself getting angrier.

'Let your father come home. You'll be taught a nice lesson for performing such dangerous experiments.' She ignored Anand's protests and left to tend to her work. In the evening, when Rajendra Prasad came home, he was told of what had transpired. 'What exactly happened? I want to hear from Anand himself,' his father announced before anyone else could say anything. Everyone looked to the boy who seemed like he was trying very hard to melt into the walls. Anand noticed his father's face was lined with wrinkles, and his moustache now had more grey than black.

'Father, the thing is, we were learning chemistry in school, and there was this equation which said if you mixed carbide with water and supply heat, you get a large amount of energy,' Anand offered.

'What "energy"? It was like a mini bomb blast,' his mother chimed in.

On the other hand, more curious than stern, his father asked him what carbide was. Having been a college graduate, he faintly remembered having studied it or heard of it, but he could not really remember what it was.

'It is a compound,' Anand answered. 'I wanted to see if the energy produced by the reaction would be enough to run a car,' Anand admitted, looking embarrassed, 'but something seems to have gone wrong.'

Rajendra Prasad nodded thoughtfully and told him that indeed, something had gone wrong.

Jayanti Devi was annoyed at her husband for not scolding their son beyond that and gave Rajendra a look. Catching the glare and remembering the initial purpose of the conversation, Rajendra wagged his finger at his son, 'Oh, oh yes, yes. Don't do such things ever again!' But if you asked Anand Kumar, he would tell you his father was not really angry at him, just extremely amused at his son's experiments. 'Just don't kill anyone,' his father joked, as soon as his mother was out of earshot, his moustache and frail body quivering with quiet laughter. 'I have high hopes for you,' Anand remembers his father saying to him one day. 'If you really want to become a scientist, you will have to study well. Mathematics is the key, as it is required in science also,' his father said as he patted his face. 'I don't know why, but I feel you will do something big.'

When he wasn't at school or studying, Anand found ways to occupy his free time that most other kids weren't interested in. While his friends were primarily drawn to sports— football and cricket in particular— Anand was more interested in experimenting and building things. He would fix his radios, and anything he saw in a book was considered fair game as an experiment. Volcanoes made of wax, model cars . . . He was always itching to try new things.

Tools were always at hand, and local technicians would supply the budding experimenter with broken gadgets like old telephone sets and dynamos. It was very evident that creating something out of nothing fascinated him.

When the kids in the mohalla were playing cricket, Anand would be devouring tattered books on science that his father bought second hand with whatever money he had to spare. On the other hand, it became more apparent as time went on that the younger sibling, Pranav, wasn't as interested in school as his older brother. Instead, he was keener on developing his talents as a musician. Pranav was following in his father's footsteps by developing his skills as a violin player. For many Indian families in the late 1970s and early 1980s, a child at school was their golden opportunity, and as technology industries began to blossom in India, so did the expectations of parents that their children should study the sciences and find a good job. Since Anand was already fulfilling the role of the eager student, this meant that Pranav was given free rein to develop his musical talents. He would go on to become a concert violinist of some renown in the Indian music scene before fate would eventually step in to change the course of his life.

Conversations in later years with his father led Anand Kumar to understand that his father was keenly aware of the poverty that had gripped his family, and his neighbours' families, for generations. He was fearful that the lack of opportunity in his native Bihar had spread its destructive tentacles over the majority of the have-nots in the state. While pockets of India were inching towards industrialization and modernity, Bihar was standing still in terms of development. Even worse was the realization that in many other ways it was marching backwards.

The public educational institutions were beginning to collapse across the state, and bloodshed arising from caste-based conflicts was once again in the news. He also did not relish the reality that so many Biharis were migrating to other states of India, and that most of them never returned.

Rajendra Prasad was convinced that Biharis were highly talented and skilled people, but that they lacked a platform to perform. From childhood he had witnessed the unpredictable games the monsoons played with the farmers. Mostly the rains were either too little or too much, only rarely did they come in the right balance. The Ganges River, too, was known to wreak devastation on its environs when the monsoons dumped their torrents of rain. Their own village had been a victim of floods on numerous occasions.

Rajendra discussed all this freely with Anand when he was growing up, and as the years rolled by and his sons grew into teenagers, he would engage them in social and political discussions over breakfast. Each morning they would divide up the newspaper and cull it for stories of interest. Then they would debate the issues.

'I began to see the world in a different way, through the eyes of my father,' Anand says. 'Today I try to read four or five newspapers every day, if possible, thanks to my father.'

✐

It wasn't until Class X that Anand Kumar began showing signs of mathematical genius, not unlike Albert Einstein, whose excellence in maths too didn't begin to emerge until he was in his mid-teens. Jayanti Devi noticed that he had started performing much better in maths, as was very evident by his high marks. His teachers too remarked on his high calibre in the subject.

Upon completing Class X, he secured admission to B.N. College in Patna. While his peers were choosing the sciences so they could some day join the engineering profession, Anand stayed on track and tackled maths as his chosen subject.

'Choose the subject that you are comfortable with,' his father advised, 'but make sure that you excel in it.'

As life went on as ever in Patna, unbeknownst to all, a student came into his own and discovered a talent innate in him.

It wasn't easy, naturally. The kind of maths he was studying by now was mostly theoretical, and overcoming the roadblocks required help. Anand's enthusiasm for his studies, his ability to solve problems, and his persistence when asking probing questions, impressed his teachers. They began to take notice of this young man who seemed to have a way with numbers, and they began to nurture his talents.

Devi Prasad Verma, one of Anand Kumar's professors at Patna University, paid attention to the promise and brilliance of this student early on.

'It was his approach that brought him closer to me,' Verma recalls. 'He was very polite, but always ready with new questions from different sources. He had a probing mind, exploring anything new in the field of mathematics by consulting journals and periodicals—not something that every young student would do.'

Professor Mohammed Shahabuddin of the Bihar College of Engineering (now NIT Patna) now leads a retired life in Patna, but back in the late 1980s and early 1990s he recalls a young student who would show up at the gates of his modest home on a regular basis to ask questions and clear doubts. It was no mean feat just to find the home in the suburbs of Phulwari Sharif, which was known for its confusing jumble of streets and lanes, but on many an evening, the professor would look out of his window and see a young man standing at his gate, a shy smile on his face barely concealing a look of expectation.

'A knock would draw my attention and I'd see Anand standing at my gate when I would open the front door. It was surprising to me, as I never encouraged students to visit my home. In fact, the first time it happened I ignored him,' he shares.

But Anand persisted, and the next night, he was at the gate again.

'I met him outside the gate . . . he had a few questions to ask about problems I had posed. I told him how to go about these and sent him away.'

But that was the start of a development that would repeat itself at least every other day, and sometimes daily, for a very long time.

'He would come to my house,' says Shahabuddin, 'and we would discuss the solutions to problems outside the gate. Satisfied, he [Anand] would return home, either by foot or by bicycle. Then, one day, impressed by his perseverance and hunger for mathematics, I called him into the house. Since then he has been like a family member to me.'

Professor Shahabuddin narrates these events with a tremendous degree of pride, though he admits that at the time he did not realize this remarkable young man would make such a splash in the world. What he did know, however, was that his student had the makings of a truly fine disciple of mathematics.

StudentSpeak

Name: Chiranjeev Kumar

Super 30 Batch: 2010

Institute and Stream: Computer Science and Engineering at IIT(BHU), Varanasi

Current Job: Adobe Systems

I did my schooling in my village till Class X. My father is a farmer and my mother used to stitch clothes, therefore my parents could afford only primary education. As my village is near the Baghmati River, it got flooded every year, and we had to live on a dam for a few months (May to July). I worked hard and got 81.8 per cent in Class X without any tuition or coaching. I wanted to get into Patna Science College but they weren't accepting students for intermediate. My dream was shattered and moreover, I had no money to study for any engineering exam. I found out about Super 30 and luckily got selected in the very first attempt. I was thrilled by Anand sir's teaching style. He used to solve a very tough maths problem using seven or eight different approaches and used to explain the solutions by involving his famous cartoon characters, Bholu and Ricky. His methodology of teaching the difficult subject is extraordinary and I became a big fan of his. The Super 30 mentorship and guidance helped me a lot, without asking for a penny, and I landed in IIT (BHU), Varanasi within the Computer Science and Engineering stream in my very first attempt. For a few months, I couldn't believe that I would have ever studied in such an awesome environment. In the four years, I focused on learning all the computer tricks, hacks, machine languages, and about the technology world. I joined Adobe Systems after college. Here, I write code to build software infrastructure to run its help website, helpx.adobe.com, most efficiently in all geographical locations and in most languages. I believe technology can change the world and people like Anand sir, who are in the mission of making this possible, are really awesome.

3

An Irreparable Loss

On a hot day in 1991, Anand was pedalling back from B.N. College on his second-hand Avon bicycle while deep in thought. On the long ride back to Chandpur Bela amid the snarls of traffic and the perpetual dust clouds that seemed to tail him, Anand had ample time to observe life in Patna and introspect on his own situation. Riding behind a private school bus, he grew sad as he watched the children from affluent families, with their shiny, happy faces, who probably had no cares except homework that loomed in front of them.

When his father had built a two-room house in Chandpur Bela in 1988, there was just one primary school in the area. In 2012, he thought gloomily, nothing had changed in spite of the population growth. The only primary school in Chandpur Bela remained quite crammed, with inadequate lighting and very limited space, to say the least. There were a few benches and desks, but not enough to go around, and while this particular school had the luxury of a blackboard on which the teacher could demonstrate lessons, it was not unusual to run out of chalk. There was no real playground at the school, just a narrow lane in front of the school which the kids made full use of to play real and imaginary games. The teachers were underpaid but strove to instil hope in a very trying environment.

The only high school was some two to three kilometres away, and lay outside of the community. Very few out of the students who actually did get there from Chandpur Bela ever graduated. Anand was the only from his neighbourhood who was currently a student at B.N. College, Patna University. Education was not considered a priority for most of the people in Anand's neighbourhood, and there was certainly no general acceptance that education would lead to greater rewards in life.

All this greatly bothered Anand. Two things plagued him constantly—how to earn a living and the lack of educational opportunities which prevailed around him. Just as he was then capable of organized thought and the means to better his situation, he truly believed that other kids could also be turned away from the vicious circle of poverty and unemployment if only they had access to proper education. An idea was beginning to form in his head as he neared his home.

Anand *knew* mathematics. He just got it. And he knew he could explain it well to others, as was evident by the many fellow students at Patna University who would seek his help to clear their doubts. After thinking long and hard over the logistics and practicalities of such an idea, Anand decided to teach students maths in return for some fee. He wanted to start a club of sorts devoted to mathematics, where students could come and learn enough to graduate from high school and perhaps go on to college.

It wasn't an original idea by any stretch of the imagination; after all, there were numerous coaching institutes spreading in Patna almost like an endemic. But the gap that Anand saw was visible in their immediate slum. There were no tutors of quality who could help teach willing students in nearby areas.

It was the same story all over Bihar. In the village of Danapur, which he visited occasionally, Anand knew of one family with twelve-year-old twins. The boys, Ravi Kumar and Arvind Kumar, rarely attended school because their father, Shambhu Rai, didn't feel it was important given the more pressing problems of earning the family's daily bread and keeping a roof over their heads. Neither Shambhu Rai nor his wife had attended school, and were likely to be illiterate all the days of their life. They raised cows and sold milk from door to door, and Shambhu felt his sons would be better off learning the family trade rather than wasting time in school.

Shambhu Rai had once told Anand that he did not feel the need to encourage his sons in that direction when he was himself already busy all day trying to eke out a living. Shambhu was a common sight in the neighbourhood, setting out on his daily rounds, carefully balancing heavy, milk-filled aluminium cans on either side of his bicycle.

Anand knew that Ravi and Arvind would spend their days playing outside or herding cows for their parents, and then one day it would be their turn to sell milk from the hard seat of a bicycle. This opportunity would then be deferred to the next generation and the shaping of this family's hopes and aspirations offered by a decent education would be further delayed.

One day, when Anand sat down with his family for breakfast, which on most days was some chilla with chutney, Anand told his father, 'We have no teachers in Chandpur Bela or close by. I think there's an opportunity for me to teach some of these kids in our backyard.' Rajendra Prasad was encouraging, and from that day they actively started talking about starting a school of some kind.

During his bicycle rides to and fro from college, the setting up of a school was all that occupied Anand's mind. He realized he'd need a premises of some kind because there was no way he could teach anyone inside their own cramped house. But where would he get money for rent? Most kids would have no money to shell out, especially at the beginning.

In any case, the first task was to find willing students. He didn't have to look far because two of his younger brother's friends, Manish Pratap Singh and Rajnish Kumar, were eager to learn and move ahead in life. Both sons of clerks, they were no strangers to the ills of poverty and were willing to work hard. With a couple of interested students, Anand then set out to find a place to teach. After some searching, he managed to convince a man he knew in the neighbourhood, Ram Narain Singh, to let him use some space in a house Singh owned. When Anand inquired about the rent, the landlord said the young man could pay him any sum when he started earning something from his fledgling enterprise.

Anand was overwhelmed, and took it as a sign that he was on the right track.

On 10 August 1992, Anand Kumar began this little maths club with two students and a classroom. The class was dedicated to the discussion of mathematics, and Anand devoted two to three hours a day, three to five days a week for many months tutoring his two students. Even some of the teachers who mentored the budding mathematician himself at Patna University began to spend time in his classroom.

What surprised Anand most was how enthusiastic the two young men were to learn. He would often have to remind himself that they were basically the same age as him, because the way they would hang on his every word indicated the opposite. Manish and Rajnish were always extremely grateful for the knowledge they were receiving, and soaked up everything that Anand and the other instructors would teach like a sponge. As a result, they did very well in their

Class XII maths examination next spring. Soon after, Anand was tutoring them for their IIT JEE exam. He immediately knew he was on to something.

Word soon got around about his little tutoring club, and the next thing Anand knew there were maths teachers and other students stopping by just to discuss mathematics problems and issues with him. His little classroom was soon a meeting place for lots of people to discuss the subject.

Manish Pratap Singh went on to complete a bachelor's degree in mathematics, and later took a shot at an engineering college entrance exam, which he did not pass. However, he was successful in securing a job with the Union Bank of India, and today is a manager at the Union Bank in Ranchi, Jharkhand. He is, without a doubt, very happy with the way his life changed after Anand decided to tutor him.

Now Manish fondly recalls the small, rented room in which the mathematics lessons would take place. It was a very humble beginning, but even in those difficult days he remembers how Anand would talk about taking his two-student school to an international level. At that time, Manish didn't think the dream would go on to become such a successful, wonderful reality. Thankful for knowing Anand's brother Pranav, he is proud of being one of the first of Anand Kumar's students and glad that he was there for the inception of the school.

The other student, Rajnish Kumar, was nineteen years old then. He knew Anand lived in a small, two-room house in Chandpur Bela with his family and didn't have any money of his own. Despite this, Anand never demanded any fees from them. They would pay very little, and only when they had the money, always thankful for their teacher's kindness and passion. Rajnish was glad not only to be part of the beginning of that extraordinary club but also knew at that early age that Anand was different from any teacher he'd had up till that point.

To make the subject interesting to them, Anand would draw connections between mathematics and real life. That was what made the difference in really getting the concepts through to his two young students.

By the time he'd completed his Class XI exam, Rajnish's grasp of the principles and language of mathematics had vastly improved. Although he made an attempt at the coveted IIT JEE, he was not fortunate enough to be accepted. Later, he went on to do a bachelor's degree in economics, and then studied law. After practising law for a short period in the Patna High Court, he moved to Mumbai to pursue a better future. Now he is a legal manager with Aegon Religare Life Insurance Company.

One mathematician influenced Anand greatly and would continue to do so as Anand's fame as a teacher grew. This man was Srinivasa Ramanujan. Anand would leap at any chance to find out more about his hero. He was very inspired by his work and realized how important Ramanujan's partnership with G.H. Hardy had been. Anand decided to name his school the Ramanujan School of Mathematics, in honour of this great Indian mathematician, who had offered such brilliant insights into the world of pure mathematics, but sadly passed away at the young age of thirty-two.

Going into 1993, word of mouth soon led to the enrolment of forty students. The classroom, which was a fifteen-by-twenty-foot hall, had a few benches and desks, but there was a good blackboard and plenty of chalk. Only students who had the means paid the nominal fees, which were about one-tenth of what other schools were charging. Anand did the bulk of the teaching, and his brother, Pranav, began handling some of the administrative aspects of the school. Paying the rent for the classroom was stressful, needless to say, but the understanding attitude of the landlord was of enormous help in those early days. Thankfully, enough students paid up regularly such that the arrears never became too large. The level of respect between landlord and tenant grew exponentially over time because the landlord realized his tenant was doing everything possible, and the tenant realized his landlord was giving him a huge opportunity to get established.

Once Anand had some income trickling in, however unsteady, he began to think about his own further education. He would pick up mathematics books sold on footpaths, usually by Russian or American authors, and pore over them in the night. He also read several biographies of famous mathematicians, including Ramanujan's, which he would read and reread for inspiration.

This was a time when the Internet did not have the ubiquitous presence it has today. There wasn't much on TV either, and newspapers also generally engaged themselves in local and national news. So most of the dreams young Anand weaved stemmed from these biographies and other books he could get his hands on. An idea was beginning to take shape in his head. In most books he read, the University of Cambridge was like the benevolent godfather that helped many geniuses discover their greatest talents. Secretly, Anand started to harbour a deep desire to attend this great institution and distinguish himself, not unlike the mathematician greats of old.

Meanwhile, Anand's younger brother Pranav moved to the Banaras Hindu University, where N. Rajam taught, for a course in playing the violin. This gave Anand an opportunity to visit his brother and discover the Central Library at BHU. The Central Library was a treasure trove. Anand read many journals of mathematics that the library subscribed to. He would make notes and attempt to solve some of the problems posed in these journals and was often immersed in one problem or the other till the librarian had to switch off the lights to get rid of him. Once, after filling almost an entire notebook trying to solve a world-class problem—several pages of scratching everything out and moving on to the next page only to attempt it again—he finally arrived at a solution. It was like stumbling in the dark, and then suddenly, someone switches the light on.

Anand worked on this result and finessed it, and then proceeded to write it down. But his writing was lacking; it was almost infantile. He took his work to Professor D.P. Verma, who was the head of the mathematics department at Patna Science College. Professor Verma helped Anand present his result better by making it publishable. Kaushal Ajitabh, a senior of Anand's by seven to eight years, was pursuing his PhD from the Massachusetts Institute of Technology

(MIT) at the time. Anand respected him greatly and sent him his paper for review. Kaushal looked the paper over and closely edited it. Both Professor Verma and Kaushal were highly impressed with the originality in thought and encouraged Anand to send it in for publication.

In 1993, after many long days and sleepless nights, a young Anand published an original paper in a prestigious British journal out of the University of Sheffield called the *Mathematical Spectrum*. The paper was titled 'Happy Numbers' and it outlined a new idea about number theory. It also heralded the arrival of a new thinker on the international mathematics scene.

Now that Anand was emerging as a mathematician of promise, Ramesh Sharma, at whose house Rajendra Prasad had stayed while studying in Patna, introduced him to Tilak Dasgupta. Dasgupta was a freelance journalist who was living in Patna at the time and wrote on poverty, unemployment and the state of inequality. It was Dasgupta who turned out to be one of the greatest influences in Anand's life. He urged Anand to find a higher purpose for his talents and abilities and not to look for personal profit.

Even now, when Anand has to take any big decisions in life, it is Tilak sir that he turns to. Anand and his wife Ritu visit Tilak Dasgupta's family in Kolkata often. So deeply entrenched is their relationship that the best moments of Anand's life today are moments he's able to spend talking to Tilak sir. Such was the impact of the man whom Anand first met in 1993.

Anand went on to publish a few more papers including one in the *Mathematical Gazette*, and his confidence increased. It was around this time that he met the editor of the Patna edition of the *Times of India*, Uttam Sengupta, through Tilak Dasgupta. There really was something about Anand—as his professor, D.P. Verma used to say, he'd only ever run across two genuine geniuses in his professional career—the first a brilliant mathematician named Vashishtha Narayan Singh (who suffered several mental breakdowns around 1993 and was later institutionalized), and the other, a young man currently studying at his college, Anand Kumar.

Anand made a distinct request to Sengupta. He wanted Sengupta to be the guest of honour at a special ceremony for the winners of a competition Anand had created to challenge his students. Sengupta was quite intrigued by the story of the Ramanujan School, and how this young student was teaching promising students himself, some at no charge. This was the beginning of a friendship that would continue for a lifetime.

The editor was initially reluctant to grant the request because, as he explained to Anand, he hadn't exactly been a shining example of mathematical prowess at school, having only scored 40 per cent in his exams in that subject. But the more they talked about

Anand's future goals to write on theoretical mathematics, the more inclined Sengupta became to be the guest of honour at the ceremony. After seeing Anand's published papers in journals, Sengupta urged Anand to apply to Cambridge. Till now, Cambridge had been only a guilty aspiration, a dream dreamed with eyes wide open—and here was a senior editor being serious about applying. Anand was reluctant, but something akin to hope tugged at him.

In April 1994, Anand filled up the application form for Cambridge, attached his published papers and sent it off without paying a single penny as application fee or anything of the sort. In the days that followed, he tried to forget about this application. *Why did I send it? All those professors must be sitting and laughing at me*, thought Anand, as he lay awake at night. *Cambridge jayenge janaab*, he derided himself.

The popularity of the Ramanujan School of Mathematics was growing and Anand was spending a lot more time with the students. Chemistry and physics were also being taught at the school now, and students were being coached for the IIT JEE entrance exams. It was remarkable how all this had happened without any advertising at a time when Patna was virtually littered with coaching institutes. One morning, while Anand was getting ready to leave for college, he heard his mother yell: *'Anand! Anand! Cambridge ka letter aaya hai!'* Jayanti Devi hurried towards him, clutching the letter in one hand and a rolling pin in the other. It had been exactly a month since he had applied. Rajendra Prasad also came in to see what the commotion was about. Anand opened the letter and handed it to his father. Anand Kumar had been accepted at Cambridge University.

Rajendra Prasad hurried out and called to Meena and his wife. Soon enough, a crowd had gathered trying to decipher exactly what news had come. *'Anand Cambridge jaayega! Cambridge!'* Laddus materialized out of nowhere and were passed around. A few children started singing, *'Anand bhaiya, maan gaye!'* Anand stood a little away from the celebrations, a wistful smile on his lips. He didn't know whether to be ecstatic or glum. Rajendra Prasad saw Anand looking forlorn in a corner and came up to him. 'What's wrong, beta? This is the best news. People in this neighbourhood didn't even know the name Cambridge, forget going there . . . what are you thinking about?'

'Father, the fee is too much. There is no way we can arrange for so much money just so I can follow my stupid dream.'

'Are you out of your mind? Do you know what this means? We all knew you had some special talent. This is your one way out of this hellhole and a chance at greatness. Do you think Ramanujan let lack of money hold him back? Don't worry. Till your father is alive, you don't have to worry about petty things like money. You concentrate on your studies, beta.' Anand, eyes shining with tears, embraced his father.

Rajendra Prasad remembered winters he'd spent studying in Patna with only cotton clothing to drape him. He made up his mind to ensure that his son had plenty of warm clothes for England. He even gave up his own coat—the only good coat he owned—and had it altered to fit Anand.

While these preparations were taking place, family and friends were stopping by in increasing numbers to wish Anand every success on his adventure. The excitement was almost palpable as the time for his departure drew near. And then fate dealt a fatal blow.

On 23 August 1994, Rajendra Prasad was taking a nap. He often slept on the floor, and on this rainy night that's where the family found him when they heard sounds of his laboured breathing. Anand and his mother rushed to assist the ailing man who was in pain and struggling to breathe. Anand dashed through the pouring rain to find someone who could help. But there was no doctor in Chandpur Bela. A compounder whom everybody called Daactar Bhagat lived some 500 metres from Shanti Kutir. Anand reached the compounder's house and beseeched him to accompany Anand home immediately. Daactar Bhagat rushed to Shanti Kutir with Anand. He examined Rajendra Prasad and declared that he was gravely ill and needed the hospital immediately as the case was beyond home care. In reality, the compounder was sure that Rajendra Prasad had passed away but he could not deliver this final news to a family who so expectantly looked at him. He urged them to take him to a doctor for confirmation. There was no taxi available so they gently laid him on a thela and Anand ran, pushing his father's prone form to the nearest hospital. It was still pouring outside.

Poor visibility, the rain, and a road full of potholes made the journey even more painful and heart-wrenching.

When they finally arrived in the emergency room at Patna Medical College, it was night. A frustrating scene awaited them. The orderlies were lounging about and no one paid attention to a soaking wet Anand with his father on a thela.

'Please, please, help me. My father is not breathing. Please save him. Please, I beg you.'

When there was no help forthcoming, a strange anger mixed with helplessness came over Anand. He became aggressive, started screaming and abusing the hospital staff. However, instead of attending to his father the staff called up the police.

It was a heartbreaking scene—a young boy who had dreams of studying at Cambridge, who still hoped that his father might live, was being dragged away by the police as he was screaming like a madman.

By now there were almost 100 people in and outside Patna Medical College who had followed Anand. They came forward and explained everything to the police and Anand was let go. The doctors checked on his father and Rajendra Prasad was declared deceased.

The journey back home was a daze. They all waited for morning, too shocked to even understand what had happened. Anand's grandmother, Shanti Devi, was in Deodaha and someone was sent during the night to bring her home on a motorcycle. They didn't tell her what awaited her in the house though.

No one could calm Shanti Devi down. She had already lost one son and to lose another was too much for her. She pulled out her hair, beat her breast and wailed continuously. There was nothing anyone could do to ease her pain.

People, who were coming to congratulate them just days before, now came to mourn with them.

At the cremation ground, Anand went through the motions as if in a trance. He performed all the rituals—all completely new and excruciatingly painful for him. He broke down when the time came to give *mukhagni*, or the ritual of putting fire into the mouth of the dead to set the pyre ablaze, performed by the eldest son as per custom. But the poor are not even allowed to mourn in peace. The priest asked Anand for money as is customary before alighting the pyre. At first, Anand in his grief didn't understand why he wasn't being allowed to proceed. When it became clear that he was expected to give some money, that same anger that bubbled over in the hospital came over him. Pranav was also greatly chagrined but tried to console his brother. 'Zaalim, they are all zaalim,' Anand cried out in anguish.

The cremation ground was packed. People had travelled all the way from Deodaha, including all of Rajendra Prasad's colleagues from the post office, as well as the neighbourhood—it seemed as if someone of note like a local politician or minister had died. The truth was that Rajendra Prasad was a much loved and respected man who had never hurt a fly. He had helped countless people over the years never expecting anything in return. There was Panditji whose beautiful son had gone missing and Rajendra had made it his personal mission to find out about his whereabouts. The young man was discovered dead from drug abuse. There was Paswan who wastes no opportunity even now to tell Anand that his father was a God. Paswan's son, Dukhharan is a labourer who used to travel to find work. When there was no news of him for a very long time, Paswan asked Rajendra Prasad to help him look for his son. Without money or means, Rajendra agreed to help. Asking people and following leads, he arrived in Benaras where he found Dukhharan missing an arm. He was pained to find that his employer wouldn't let him go back to the village as he was afraid there would be trouble because of this accident caused at the construction site. In the end, Rajendra was able to bring Dukhharan back.

This anecdote is especially telling because Anand seems to have inherited some of his father's nature. If he is able to work for the poor and not for personal gain it is because that is the kind of heart he has seen since he was a very young child. Rajendra didn't care that he had no money to help people or that he got no fame or fortune out of it; he didn't think he was doing anything special by taking care of an ageing woman in their house who was of no relation to him. As a young man, he would spend time with her and attend to her needs as she was completely bedridden. Even in an atmosphere where caste and creed were of the utmost importance, he developed a sign language to communicate with a mute woman across the house who belonged to a different caste. He was able to rise above these differences and see human beings for who they really were: essentially the same.

Back home that day, Anand lay on the floor, his brother next to him, and he saw a sliver of the coat his father had given him hanging inside the room. With a jolt, Anand realized that the gift had been given less than twenty-four hours before. He vowed that he would not wear it till he was worthy of the coat.

StudentSpeak

Name: Nidhi Jha

Super 30 Batch: 2013–14

Institute and Stream: Civil Engineering, Indian School of Mines

Current Job: Student

I'm eighteen now and I was sixteen when all of this started. IIT JEE: the big dream. I had heard of Super 30 and Anand sir's charm and I got my chance to witness it in the year I dropped out to prepare for JEE. I'm basically a resident of Varanasi and I currently study in the Indian School of Mines (ISM), Dhanbad, an institute currently in the process of being converted into an IIT.

I belong to a family of four sisters and a brother. My father drives a rented autorickshaw and mother is a housewife. As we know, education is the biggest market these days and coaching is really expensive; but Super 30 came to my rescue. Anand sir has been a constant inspiration to all of us. Every time somebody felt low, he was the one to lift them up. He is the idol of my life. It was because of him that I could muster the courage to stay well through the entire year. Even his family, especially Pranav sir, is very supportive and has always treated all of us as one of their own.

I'd just like to add that I owe my life to that man and I consider Super 30 and Anand sir the most integral and special parts of my life.

4

Papad-wallah Ladka

It was hard to come out of the pall of grief that enveloped Shanti Kutir. Anand's friends and relatives pressed him to continue the search for funds to go to Cambridge. He approached his friend Uttam Sengupta, who helped in putting out word through the *Times of India*. A professor of Hindi from Patna University came forward and arranged a meeting for Anand with a minister in Patna. The minister was positive and asked for Anand to see him at 11 a.m. the next day.

Anand arrived on time, but was swiftly stopped at the gates.

'The minister has called me at 11 a.m. to talk about my Cambridge plans,' Anand explained.

After several more questions, he was allowed to proceed and then made to wait outside in the lobby. After another half hour, he was led inside a large room. Anand was taken aback at entering the room. He was expecting a one-on-one chat with the minister but there were several neta-types in the room, all talking loudly and engaged in what was a boisterous discussion.

'*Aao Anand, aao. Baitho, baitho beta,*' the minister welcomed Anand smilingly and gestured to him to sit on a chair in one corner of the room. Anand understood that the minister would tend to him shortly as there were important matters being discussed.

At first he tried to be inconspicuous but soon he registered the statements flying around.

'The seat should not be given to him. Instead we should go for . . . '

'Yes yes, he has a large caste-based vote bank. He would be much better.'

Anand sat listening, scarcely believing what he was hearing. *I spend my time over mathematics equations but here these politicians are churning out such complicated caste equations!* Anand was aghast.

He waited for fifteen to twenty minutes, and then politely called attention to himself. 'Sir, you had called me to discuss my Cambridge plans . . . '

'Yes, of course. I call everybody who studies hard and has our state's best interests at heart. I respect them and encourage them,' the minister said loftily, in a loud voice, raising his arms. And he turned his attention again to the campaign management that the netas were discussing.

Anand nervously thought, *Minister saab is not getting the hint about the money. Maybe I should be more direct.*

'Yes sir,' Anand interrupted again, 'but like the professor discussed with you, I need some financial help.'

'Yes, I spoke about monetary help. But the best of the best are destroyed at the altar of money. Do not pursue money. Keep on doing good karma, you'll get everything,' and once again he turned to the room at large.

After another fifteen minutes or so Anand finally said, 'Sir, do not mind. But I need some money to go to Cambridge.'

'Yes, go to America, go to London, go to the best institutes. Study hard! But come back to this land of Buddha and Mahavira. I had called you just to tell you this. Don't forget, beta, your country needs you.'

Anand understood that there was no concrete help coming his way and left.

Anand walked out, his head hung low. Across the road from the minister's bungalow, he saw a chai stall and rummaged in his pockets and found a few rupees. He decided to have a cup of tea and collect his thoughts. The chai-wallah looked at the young man holding on to a bundle of certificates with his head in his hands, and asked him, *'Kya hua? Kis kaam se gaye the Minister saab ke paas? Naukri ke liye?'* Hopeless and weary, Anand related the entire story to the sympathetic stranger. 'Money? Which idiot professor sent you? They have not paid me for tea for four months now, what financial help will they give you? They are of no use. Give up your dreams and find a job.' Anand stared into his cup of tea and deeply pondered the chai-wallah's words.

Anand was dejected. Even with his father by his side, he had faced such dead ends. Some people had told his father about a religious organization which sends a handful of students to England for training and takes care of all expenses. So the father-son duo had gone to the organization to learn more about the procedure. First, they said you will have to convert to this religion, then change your name, and complete some legal formalities. Then, they said, you come to us with your application.

It is commonly said that Bihar and UP are entrenched in casteism; all politics is caste-based and vote banks are of utmost importance. So some people suggested to Rajendra Prasad to go to the leader of their caste and he would surely help. They had a successful meeting with this leader and he said that the money would be arranged in a couple of days. Rajendra Prasad and Anand were ecstatic. They went back to see the leader a couple of days later.

'Yes, the money is being arranged. You will have to marry your son to the daughter of a very rich man. Don't worry, they are of the same caste. The money will come as dowry.' Disgusted, Rajendra Prasad led his son away.

After his father's death, Anand received a letter from a man who had read about him in

The Hindu. He said he was a rich businessman in Delhi and invited Anand home to meet with him. Anand, spending his own money, bought a general class ticket and travelled to Delhi. On reaching Safdarjung Enclave, he was warmly welcomed, served tea and had a brief but heartening meeting with the businessman. But on his return, he called and called the Delhi businessman but sadly in vain.

Nobody comes to your aid when you really need help. All these voluntary organizations, NGOs, they are no good. They only want to help people who get them publicity, Anand thought bitterly.

Uttam Sengupta went to bat for Anand once more by approaching Lalu Prasad Yadav. Anand went to meet him but was stopped by the secretary. The secretary asked him to write down his purpose of visit on a piece of paper and told him that Laluji was not available. It was slowly becoming apparent that his hope of going to Cambridge had died with his beloved father.

Jayanti Devi would watch Anand return home day after day without scoring any luck, and her heart would sink further. She was struggling to put food on the table with the meagre pension she received from the postal office, yet still, she kept pushing Anand to not give up hope. One evening, when Anand returned home she said to him, 'I have decided. You sell this jewellery I have and get in exchange whatever money it's worth. You and Pranav are my real jewels; what will I do with this useless metal?' Anand was overcome with emotion and he tried to laugh off her offer, 'Don't be silly, ma. These metals hardly have any worth, save emotional. There's no way they would cover the cost for Cambridge. Come, let's eat and forget about all this for a while.' But when they sat down to dinner, there were only rotis. Money for the month was running out. Also, unlike in some cases when in the case of a young death the government provides compensation, it emerged that there was a cooperative loan that Rajendra Prasad had taken, among others, to build the house. The family was to pay back an amount of Rs 18,000. It was then that Anand made up his mind to bury the Cambridge dream and shoulder the responsibility to take care of his family.

The Ramanujan School of Mathematics was temporarily shut down because it took so much of the brothers' time and yielded hardly any income. The immediate priority was to earn money, or they would be starving for want of two square meals a day. Jayanti Devi decided on a plan of action. She had never worked outside the home, and until her husband's demise, her world had revolved around being the perfect homemaker. She diligently attended to the needs of her family, visited her neighbours, family and friends routinely, and prayed in her spare time. She was not skilled in any other occupations, but she was an accomplished cook, and was well known for her papads, which she made from scratch. She proposed that she could make papads and they could sell it at a marginal profit. Anand agreed.

Papad is usually made of rice or lentils. Jayanti Devi would grind dry black lentils into a powder, and then make the dough by adding water, salt and spices. The dough would then be flattened into very thin sheets with a rolling pin, and the paper-thin pieces were later dried in the sun. It was back-breaking work as they did all the kneading by hand and then steady vigilance was required as even one gust of wind could have an entire batch flying off the terrace, where they were left out to dry. They were also very brittle and had to be handled with care, as the shopkeepers would reject the broken papads. In some time Jayanti, with some help, was making hundreds of papads a day. They also made cow-dung cakes that acted as cooking fire fuel for the vadas or lentil fritters.

As the delivery man, Anand would run through the streets and lanes to sell the family's labour to shopkeepers. By day he sold papads, by night he studied. His mother would beseech him to shut his books and get some sleep. This kind of work did not come naturally to Anand. Social inhibitions and an early reticence made the papad business somewhat uncomfortable for the young scholar, but necessity proved more compelling and, in time, he came to like the business.

Anand would mount his bicycle early in the morning with the papads tied securely on the back seat. He would then do his rounds. Many of the shopkeepers took to the winsome youth readily enough—especially when they became aware of the family tragedy—but others were not so kind and treated him poorly. He came to be called the 'papad-wallah ladka' by the shopkeepers. Since distribution and manpower were their greatest limitations, Anand realized that he would have to lean on personal resources and leverage relationships with shopkeepers to earn a living. It wasn't easy but he was not deterred by a sharp word or a cutting remark. He quickly learned the great challenges that every businessperson faces, and began to develop the thick skin that serves him well till now.

The revenues from the papad business were not spectacular, but they gradually replaced the income that Rajendra Prasad had provided to the family. In a year or two, they were able to pay off the Rs 18,000 loan. Still, the work was hard, especially for Jayanti, and it took its toll on everyone.

Meena Prasad, whom Anand, Pranav and Om all called Guruji, had moved from Shanti Kutir a couple of years before Rajendra Prasad's passing. He had decided to move a little farther away to a drier area. Now things have changed, but in those days Chandpur Bela would get flooded during the monsoon and there would be knee-deep water in the streets for weeks on end. It was very difficult for a disabled man who had difficulty walking to navigate in such situations. One of the boys would hoist Guruji upon his shoulders and wade through the water, but it was clear that he needed a place which was safe and dry. So it was that Guruji moved with Chachiji, his wife, to modest quarters a little higher up on land, and their son Om would go back and forth between the two houses. Chachiji, as Anand and Pranav called her, would try to arrange for a few rupees and sometimes make vegetables for the boys when they were sick of eating dal and bhaat.

After the family tragedy, Om Kumar too was very much a part of the desperate struggle to make money. While growing up, no one could tell which son belonged to which set of parents. There was no distinction between the three. Anand and Pranav called Uncle Meena Guruji, and so did Om. Pranav and Om were in the same class in school, Om being just four months younger than Pranav. The three brothers remained thick through the years—Om and Pranav especially were quite the inseparable duo. But where Anand was the studious one and Pranav Kumar was musically inclined, Om started to fall into a bad crowd as he grew up. He stopped studying and started hanging around with the other slum children. With them, he would smoke bidis and ganja, and eat khaini. One day, a little before his Class X exams, Rajendra Prasad confronted him: 'You're like a son to me. Why are you wasting away your life? I have never treated you any different from Anand and Pranav.

What did I do wrong?' Saying this, he broke down. Seeing Rajendra Prasad in tears jolted Om into guilt; he hadn't meant to hurt him. In fact, all his life Om had called Rajendra *pitaji*, just as Anand and Pranav had. Om realized the pain he was causing his family. He promised Rajendra Prasad, '*Aaj ke baad main aapko shikayat ka mauka nahi doonga, pitaji. Main sab galat kaam chhodd doonga.*' He began afresh. He studied very hard. But even after studying diligently, he wasn't able to score well in his Class X exams. But everyone saw that he had tried assiduously.

Rajendra Prasad told him to learn typing. Back in those days, learning how to type was a good way to increase your employability skills. After Rajendra Prasad passed away, Om grieved silently. The man who had inspired him was no more. He started to learn typing in earnest, but like his two brothers, was forced to throw himself into the papad business as well. Anand observed how Om would go to college in the morning, then spend four to five hours practising his typewriting skills, and then go off on a delivery route, different from Anand's, to distribute papads.

In 1997–98, Om's hard work finally paid off. As pitaji had predicted, he cleared the Staff Selection Commission (SSC) exam in the very first attempt and landed a job as a stenotypist in Allahabad. He continued his training there and today is an accounts officer of the Government of India in Patna.

✎

The months passed, and the papads were helping to pay the bills . . . though not quite enough to keep hunger away from their door completely. There were nights when Anand and his brother went hungry. When there was food, they'd sit cross-legged on the floor of their home with their mother and scarf down the simple roti and vegetables with gusto. On those days, when his mother could put together his favourite egg curry and chapattis, Anand was in heaven. When there was no food, however, Anand would gulp down a glass of cold water and try to ignore the hunger that was a way of life for many in Bihar.

For the first time in his life, Anand truly understood the devastating psychological impact of hunger—more potent than the physical effects. He came to realize how fortunate his family had been to have the measly salary his father had earned from the postal department. He also began to realize why some people did what they did to escape the clutches of hunger.

In his weaker moments, Anand thought about moving to Mumbai or Kolkata to earn a decent living. But every time he pictured leaving his mother and home, he felt hollow. *I can't do it. It would be like cutting off my arm and going on with life*, thought Anand.

Anand began to think his academic aspirations had died a slow death. *I am an educated man. If we go on trying to make ends meet with back-breaking work, where will we get to in life? What is the point of education, if you cannot do something better?*

The margins from the papad business were low, but it was a steady income. Anand reasoned with himself and realized that they needed to keep it afloat. But almost a year after he'd shut the Ramanujan School of Mathematics, he also began to toy with the idea of reopening it. His family was encouraging and his mother said that it was what his father would have wanted. Anand knew it too. Rajendra Prasad would have never wanted the school to be shut down.

Anand decided to take the bull by the horns and attempted another shot at teaching. He reopened the Ramanujan School of Mathematics in 1995. Anand used up some of the money they had made from selling papads to contribute towards rent. The initial response was less than inspiring, with just six students enrolling in the programme. But this didn't discourage Anand; on the contrary, he felt all the thoughts which tormented him simply fell to the side. He felt fearless in the classroom, in front of all his students. The worrying was shunted to the back of his mind, and he put all his passion and determination into teaching his six students. In the classroom, Anand was transformed.

Anand's students liked both what he taught and the way he taught. His teaching was clear and insightful, and they found the assignments enabled them to start solving mathematics problems on their own, with little difficulty. It wasn't long after that word spread that the young teacher was wielding his magic again.

A few of the students at Ramanujan were serious about tackling the IIT JEE exam and other competitive engineering exams. However, the fees that the coaching institutes demanded were exorbitant, and there was no way these students could afford them. Anand decided to coach them at just a tenth of what they were expected to pay elsewhere. Anand's tuition system was unbelievably simple: You could pay in whatever way that was convenient to you; you could pay whenever you had money— none of the advance, upfront payments that were so hard to comply with for the less fortunate.

Anand would run deliveries in the morning and use the cycling time to prep for his classes in the evening. It was certainly unorthodox, but he was able to pick anecdotes and examples that were rooted in reality and struck a chord with the students.

It was around this time that Anand regularly began to create mathematical quizzes aimed at young readers for the *Times of India*, an assignment which materialized out of his growing familiarity with Uttam Sengupta. Uttam remained a staunch believer

Anand Kumar as a toddler with his father, Rajendra Prasad.

Anand with his parents, Rajendra Prasad and Jayanti Devi.

Anand at the inauguration of the Ramanujan School
of Mathematics in Mithapur on 10 August 1992.

Anand sharing a light moment with
the students of the first batch in 1992.

Anand in the classroom with the
second batch in 1993.

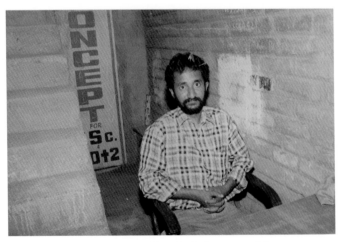

Pranav Kumar at the small makeshift venue of the institute
at B.M. Das Road, Patna, during the initial period in 1996.

Checking the IIT JEE result with
Super 30 students in 2005.

The proud Super 30 students after clearing the IIT JEE entrance
in 2011 with Lok Sabha Speaker Meira Kumar.

Anand being offered puris by his students.

Super 30 students in their hostel where they study hard night and day.

Students taking the Super 30 entrance test.

The Super 30 batch of 2010, with Anand and Pranav, celebrating at India Gate after shooting for a TV programme.

Anand giving a motivational speech.

Anand addressing the Department of Education of the German
state of Saxony with Eva-Maria Stange, minister of state for
higher education and research.

Recognition for Super 30 over the years.

in Anand's oeuvre and would always have moral support to offer the young man, at the very least. It became a very popular column in the daily newspaper at that time, and was carried on a weekend pull-out called *Career and Competitions*, which targeted students specifically. This, combined with the word of mouth of students at the Ramanujan School stoked Anand's popularity, and the rate of enrolment picked up. By 1996, there were thirty-six students at the school.

With the school burgeoning, the financial restraints faced by Anand's family began to slowly ebb away. Every successful student's story brought new young people to the school looking to study, and between the papad business and the tuition fees, there was now a bit of money to afford the necessities of life.

As the number of students kept growing, Anand discovered he needed more room, so he moved the location of the school to a larger premises in Rajendra Nagar in central Patna.

It was a very shrewd move from a business perspective because now the school was located in an area that made it easier to get to, and thus likely to attract more students. It was a new beginning, as central Patna was the hub of coaching institutes in those days, and with the new location, exceptional teaching and very low fees, students from poor communities began seeking out the Ramanujan School of Mathematics.

Meanwhile, Pranav, who was advancing his career as a violinist in Mumbai, would keep coming to Patna to take care of the administrative side of things. They hired a few teachers to tackle physics and chemistry for students, which naturally added to the overhead costs, and made Pranav's responsibilities that much more valuable as a careful accounting of the school's financial resources had to be maintained if everyone and everything was to be taken care of, and if the school was going to be a long-term success.

By 1997, the student population at the Ramanujan School was more than 300. The classrooms were cramped, but it only added to the sense of camaraderie and bonding that these students enjoyed. Other coaching institutes were stumped as to how every IIT JEE aspirant was knocking on the door of Ramanujan. One of the reasons was the way Anand personally involved himself in the students' study lessons. Despite the large number, Anand knew every student by their first name, and he knew each student's capacity to learn and eventual goals. Every student received personal attention from him, and they knew they could talk to him about pretty much anything. It wasn't just mathematics that the students were learning, but lessons about life, its challenges and possible solutions—these were not lessons that could be bought with a hefty fees.

Anand continued to add to the facilities year on year, always striving to improve the quality of teaching imparted. He purchased a public address system that included several speakers and installed them at every corner of the school to address the large gatherings of students that congregated each day . . . as many as 300 at a time on many an occasion. He would himself stand on a raised platform that was built so that the students could see him clearly. The blackboard that he used to draw equations and diagrams on was always behind him, with plenty of chalk. The students were attentive, he was enthusiastic, and the results spoke volumes.

By 1998, Anand was swamped with work. The student population had grown a third by then, and having to teach more than 400 students had both its rewards and its challenges.

That same year, Anand was to travel to IIT Kanpur. From Delhi, he telephoned Uttam Sengupta who was then posted in Lucknow as the editor of the *Times of India*. He was keen to make a stop in Lucknow to see this friend who had been such an unflinching support in his times of struggle. He arrived late in the evening at Sengupta's house and first took a much-needed shower as he was exhausted from the train travel. While his guest was showering, Sengupta noticed two bags full of books that Anand had brought with him. Out of curiosity, he looked at the books and was pleasantly surprised to find that each of the books was a foreign-published tome about mathematics—a rather expensive luxury for a poor papad-seller from the slums of Gaudiya Math. When Anand came out, Sengupta pointed at these bags and asked him how he had managed to afford them. Anand simply replied, 'Money I made from the school.' There were 400 students enrolled in Ramanujan and each student paid Rs 500 a year which amounted to Rs 2,00,000 rupees in a year. After paying the staff, rent for the school, plus other overheads, there was still a sizeable amount left.

Now there was a steady income, and starvation no longer clawed at their doors. But this security came at a cost. Everyone, Anand in particular, was exhausted at the end of the day. He was still delivering papad in the morning and then teaching for several hours in the afternoon and evening. He was also still studying mathematics in his very limited free time. One evening, Jayanti Devi was helping him pack the papads that he had to deliver. Anand could barely keep his eyes open, and his face was ashen. She touched his forehead with her hand, and it was burning up.

'You cannot go on like this!' she told him.

'I'm fine, ma,' he brushed her off.

'You are twenty-five years old and nearing a collapse. I will not have it. What good is this money if something happens to you?' she said, sweat glistening on her face.

After some long, difficult discussions with the rest of the family, they decided to give up the papad business to concentrate on the school.

By 2000, the school had approximately 500 pupils on the student rolls. It was by far the most successful institute in Patna based on its achievement rates. Students who received the excellent coaching and fine-tuning that the Ramanujan School had to offer were cracking the IIT JEE and other exams more frequently than students from other institutions.

It was also an open secret that some of these institutions together were like an informal coaching mafia and were not above using intimidation and violence to get what they wanted. Unfortunately for Anand, schools owned by members of the coaching mafia were amongst those hardest hit by the success of this newcomer to the scene. Some institutions got it into their heads that something had to be done about this 'problem' if their schools were to survive.

A pattern of intimidation began in 2000 against Anand, the school, and the school's landlord, a Bengali woman who rented the premises to the Ramanujan School. An attempt was made to usurp the title to the prime land on which the school was located and later, a civil case was also filed against the landlord and the school, the details of which were murky. Local police joined hands with the persecutors and once even pulled Anand out on the street and ordered him to vacate the school premises immediately. When the young teacher refused, he was arrested and taken to the local police station.

When Anand's students got wind of the situation, they arrived at the police station in large numbers and eventually forced their way in, demanding that their beloved teacher be released and further demanding to know why he had been arrested. Anand was finally released from police custody with no charges, but this was far from the end of his woes.

Not known to walk away quietly, the coaching mafia made sure things came to a head in July 2000. Three goons armed with guns opened fire on the school and hurled crudely fashioned bombs in an effort to create panic. Once again, it was Anand's students who came to the rescue. They stormed out of the school and took the thugs by surprise. The pent-up fury, against those who had been trampling on them since they were born, poured out, and quickly the students managed to physically restrain two of the three goons. Anand called the police and the attackers were handed over.

A semblance of calm returned, but the hostility from the coaching mafia was still palpable. The land issue was proving to be a real problem as the Bengali landlord was beginning to feel the pressure, and she was no longer that keen to have Anand's school located on her property. With 500 pupils, the building was also proving to be too small, and there wasn't anything nearby which would serve the purpose as adequately. The safety of his students was also of utmost importance, especially in the wake of the bombing attempt.

After much hunting, Anand finally discovered a large area located in a secluded part of town that was often waterlogged, on the outskirts of Patna near Kumhrar. They filled up the waterlogged area with sand and rocks and soon made it habitable. This new location was a risk because he was moving away from a prime location in the heart of the coaching district, and some felt students wouldn't travel that far to study.

For his part, despite the odds, Anand was confident his teaching abilities would keep students coming, and in the end he was right. They would wade through knee-high water during the rainy season to attend his classes. In his mind, and perhaps in theirs, his classroom had literally become an oasis of learning for his poor students. The new location didn't slow down the Ramanujan School in the least, and the surge of new students proved the point.

As time passed, demand remained high, but Anand felt anything more than 500 students would become unfeasible for the school because of limited space and resources. It was time to figure out a way to limit enrolment, and after discussing it with the other teachers, it was decided that an entrance exam was the only way to achieve the desired goal. In the very first exam, an astounding 7500 students sat for the test.

There were some who tried to 'influence' the results with bribes, but Anand and Pranav were unrelenting in their determination to ensure that merit alone would be the deciding factor at the Ramanujan School. The bribes were refused, in spite of the huge difference it would have made to their family situation, and the tuition fees were kept deliberately low so that even poor students could afford to attend. In extreme cases of poverty, tuition was simply waived for bright students who showed potential.

By the end of 2000, the Ramanujan School had firmly settled into its new location. It was far from perfect—there was water everywhere, the buildings were at best walls with a roof, and the tools for teaching were limited—but its 500 students weren't there for the aesthetics. No, they were there to learn, to achieve high marks, to get coached for their post-secondary institute examinations, and to pass those tests. They were willing to bear it all to be taught by a brilliant mathematician who taught phenomenally well, cared for his students, and did whatever was necessary to see them through to achieving their dreams.

Life seemed to be on track for Anand. What more could a poor family from Bihar ask for? They had sufficient money, and things were looking up. Little did they know that Anand Kumar's conscience sat uneasy, and before long, a series of events would tip the scale over and reveal what this unassuming man was capable of.

StudentSpeak

Name: Mohammed Aquibur Rahman

Super 30 Batch: 2008

Institute and Stream: Mining Machinery
Engineering, ISM Dhanbad; IIM Ahmedabad

Current Job: Marketing Manager, *Cardekho.com*

Brad Henry said, 'A good teacher can inspire hope, ignite the imagination, and instil a love of learning.' The description best suits Anand sir who didn't just make me visualize mathematical concepts but also helped me dream big and inspired me to achieve them. Coming from an area and a community with high illiteracy rates, my family or I could never imagine I'd be where I am now. The way Anand sir always focuses on the basics and the way he uses humour and interactivity in the classroom, it is so easy for me to recall any mathematical concept even now. Anand sir, apart from teaching maths in a beautiful way, imparts a lifetime of learning in his classroom, which inspires one to fight and struggle to achieve one's goal without being distracted by the difficulty of a situation and time. He himself is a role model for the underprivileged and the downtrodden. He is the one who instils the confidence in his students that we can achieve anything no matter what the circumstances might be.

5

A Force Called Super 30

In early 2002, a young boy named Abhishek Raj came to the Ramanujan School of Mathematics. Accompanied by his mother, Abhishek told Anand that he was keen to join the school to study for the IIT entrance exam but he would not be able to pay the fee immediately. He said that he would pay Anand instalments as and when his father made a little money from harvesting potatoes. His mother hastened to add that Abhishek was a very good student and used to come first in every class in the village school.

127

The fee in those days was a paltry Rs 1000 for a year. However, Anand made the boy and his mother sit down and tell him more about their story.

Abhishek was from a small village called Rasalpur in Bihar. His father was a poor farmer and unemployed except for the measly return he would get when the potato crop he laboured for was not ruined by the errant monsoons. Abhishek went to school in the village and studied diligently, unmindful of the fact that not only were there were no chairs or tables in the school, but even the doors and windows had been pilfered. Abhishek's father couldn't afford to buy books or put his son in a small private school. But his mother, Sudha Kumari, was an educated woman. She tried to find work as a tutor, which was hard in Rasalpur, but eventually she did manage to earn a measly Rs 100 every month through tutoring. A pittance, but she had no choice even though she was clearly underpaid.

Anand was stunned that Sudha Kumari had educated her son by working so hard and that too, despite earning so little. He told them that he was starting a new programme and asked them to come again next week.

The truth was that this was not the first time Anand had come across such a pitiable case.

A boy by the name of Kishan Kumar had also come to see Anand. Barefoot and in a tattered shirt, he told Anand that he wanted to be an engineer but had no money for the tuition fees.

'Where do you live in Patna?' Anand asked him.

'I look after a rich man's house and he lets me stay for free. But I'm not a chowkidar,' he said defiantly. 'I came to Patna to become an engineer. I study every day.'

Anand was a bit sceptical so he asked for the address of this man's house and decided to have a look-see for himself. In the evening he went to the house. He saw Kishan Kumar sitting near the gate with a book in his hand. It was dark and he was studying by the light of the street lamp. His heart almost broke.

Anand was in turmoil. *When I needed money to go to Cambridge, no one helped me. What is the point of my school if I can't help bright kids whose only fault is being born in poverty?* This particular case haunted him. He realized there must be many more like Kishan Kumar or even Abhishek Raj who could not afford even the requisite Rs 1000 a year for coaching. Why wasn't he thinking about them?

Father would have expected more of me. Even if my students are doing well, at the end of the day I'm providing them a service in return for a fee, he thought.

That's not true, a voice in his head, which sounded uncannily like his mother's, countered. *You do much more than merely teach. You help hundreds of students beyond the call of duty, and charge a bare minimum!*

But you have a higher purpose. Don't forget, Rajendra Prasad's voice resounded in Anand's head.

'Great. Now, I'm going mad too. What a mahaan teacher I am,' Anand shook his head trying to clear his thoughts. But as he walked back home, he decided that he would put himself out there and do something to help and uplift those who couldn't afford proper education. And as always, the idea that he toyed with whenever he had some headspace came back to him. Except this time, Anand felt that he needed to share the dream with his family and bring it to fruition.

'We cannot feed thirty students for free! What are you? A sant mahatma?' said Jayanti Devi.

Anand had poured his heart out to Pranav and Jayanti Devi. Now that he had some money, he wanted to make a real difference to fight poverty. Ever since his Cambridge dream had been so cruelly shelved, Anand empathized with and often thought about the million opportunities that evaded students only because they weren't born into money. He wanted to do something for such students but unfortunately, so far, he had never had the means. Now that there was a steady trickle of income, Anand couldn't stop thinking about diversifying the Ramanujan School and devoting himself to those who couldn't even afford the paltry sums that the school asked.

He decided that he would hold an entrance exam for underprivileged students to test their potential. Out of these, he would pick the top thirty students and prepare them for the IIT JEE free of cost. Not only that, he would house the students nearby (he wasn't sure how at the moment). He was just requesting his mother, by way of discussion, if she would cook for all his students in her kitchen, as it would be too expensive to cater food from outside for their meals. Anand had arrived at the number thirty after much pondering—fifty would have been beyond their means but he felt thirty was a number they could strive towards.

'Ma, think about it. You have seen the power of education. We are able to live comfortably now only because pitaji worked hard to educate us. A man without money has only one way to escape his misfortune— education. You educate one boy, you elevate an entire village.'

His mother looked at him with pride, but tried not to show it: 'You think you are Superman! How do you plan to achieve this?' Pranav, who had been listening in the whole time, piped up, 'Bhaiya, maybe you should name them Super 30.' When Jayanti Devi saw that they were quite set on the

133

idea, she said, 'Fine. I will see what I can do.' Anand got up and touched her feet. He knew that she would be a key part of this crusade.

Thanks to his mother's outburst, the name Super 30 stuck. Pranav was completely behind Anand's initiative. He vowed to take care of the administrative part of the programme and urged Anand to concentrate on preparing the coursework and selection criteria instead. There were logistics that needed to be figured out though. They would need a place where they could house thirty students.

'Why can't it be a day school, bhaiya? Why do we need to make sure all the students stay with us?' Pranav asked Anand.

'I don't want our students to be limited to Patna. Students who come from poor villages in Bihar would not be able to afford accommodation in Patna. They will only be able to study if they don't have to worry about money,' Anand said.

Anand felt very strongly about his fast-developing idea. Also, though he didn't say it to Pranav then, Anand felt that they needed to be separated from the dismal conditions of their everyday lives and given a safe environment in which to study. He wanted these children under his supervision because he anticipated that they would need a lot of counselling and confidence-building if they were to do well, in school and in life.

In the spring of 2002, a small shack with a tin roof was set up next to Anand's own home. They fashioned a blackboard out of wood, basic wooden benches and desks were installed, and a classroom was ready.

Next, they had to find living accommodations for the thirty students, which was not as easy. Early in their search they found various places around Shanti Kutir where groups of students could stay.

(In later years, they would make a bare-bones hostel to accommodate the students, as Anand realized that it made sense to have the entire bunch live in close quarters to each other.) To top it off, a medical practitioner who was Anand's friend, Dr B.K. Prasad, agreed to treat student ailments, should they arise, free of charge.

Super 30, a wild and crazy experiment, was going to become a reality—slowly, it began to sink in.

It was agreed that Anand's mother, Jayanti Devi, would make the meals two times a day for these Super 30 students in a small kitchen in a corner of the hut, where pans and cooking utensils were stored after some scrounging. The meals would be basic but nutritious; students wouldn't have a hungry stomach distracting them from their studies.

Pranav would be the business manager and supervisor for the project, while the obvious choice for the instructor was

Anand himself. Needless to say, it was a skeletal project, but Anand's infectious enthusiasm was caught by everybody. He was confident that expenses for the programme could be covered by proceeds from the Ramanujan School of Mathematics, and he did not solicit donations, nor accept those that were offered. Yes, people were willing to help, but Anand was convinced that the Super 30 project needed to avoid any possible accusations of corruption if it were to succeed, and the best way to do that was not to accept money from anyone, regardless of the source. It wasn't so much pride as a determination to show the young people under his tutelage that money was not the only factor that determined a person's worth in society. If they were going to succeed, they were going to have to do so through hard work alone.

The most important thing was devising an appropriate test that let them identify thirty deserving candidates. Anand and his team were determined that only the brightest and neediest would be able to take advantage of the Super 30 opportunity. The determining factors would be natural aptitude, a desire to learn, and a willingness to work hard, regardless of the circumstances. Through the years, Anand had seen many bright students travel to Patna in search of a quality education, only to be forced to return to their villages because they had no money and subsequently couldn't find the right opportunity for them. It was these kids he had in mind when he first floated the concept of the Super 30 project.

A few times, Anand would pause in whatever he was doing and find himself thinking, *Can this really work? Right now everyone is excited and involved in getting this off the floor, but will it be too much? What if it fails horribly? What if they are unable to get along and stay together? I am after all going to be responsible for these thirty students' well-being.* And so on and so forth.

But despite his reservations, something kept propelling him forward. He thought of his father's coat, which Rajendra Prasad had lovingly altered to fit his son. Anand wanted to become a man worthy of that coat. He thought, *Even if four or five students pass the examination, it's better than nothing. They have nothing to lose. So I have nothing to lose either.*

Anand set to work on the selection test, and the initial screening process was put in place. The test included thirty questions in all—ten each for physics, chemistry, and maths. They were objective-type questions with a single correct choice, and based on the level of the NCERT syllabus. They let students of the Ramanujan School know about this programme and asked them to spread the word amongst their peers. The test was scheduled for May and hundreds of candidates applied for the thirty spots available in the Super 30 programme.

In the early years of the programme, the exam was relatively easy to administer, but over the past seven or eight cycles, it has become increasingly elaborate as more and more students from all over northern India attempt to join Super 30. In 2002, there was only one exam location, but today exams are held in multiple centres throughout northern India, including Patna, Benares, Delhi and elsewhere. The fee to take the examination is set very low at Rs 50 per candidate, with the money going towards the rentals of the exam halls, printing of the question papers, and other incidentals. There is almost no profit from the examinations.

Anand and a few trusted others sifted through the tests to find out who'd make up the very first batch of Super 30. Twenty days later, a paper was taped on to the gate of Shanti Kutir. Thirty names were written by hand on it. The results were out. So it had begun.

Classes began shortly after the notice was posted to the front gate. The students arrived to find they had places to sleep, regular meals and daily classes. Time management was the first lesson the students had to learn because there was so little time and so much to do before the exams. The IIT JEE was exactly one year away, and every minute was going to count if these eager, young students were going to get in.

Initially, most of the students found it difficult to deal with the new environment. There was very little contact with their families and most felt uncomfortable being in an unfamiliar place.

Another unsettling factor was the other unknown students and faculty. Like any group of strangers that is brought together, it took the students and staff of Super 30 some time to establish a rhythm and get over the initial shyness. Luckily, they all had a common purpose, and there was too little time to worry about all this.

Staying out of trouble wasn't difficult for the Super 30 class. There was little in the way of entertainment, and most of the students didn't have the money or time to afford distractions anyway. The only exceptions were India vs Pakistan cricket matches; then they would evade Anand and try and follow the score however they could. Studying late into the evening was necessary to keep up with the curriculum and to be ready for the next day's challenges, and so they didn't have much free time to kill. Not only was there self-study to do, but the students also barely had time to deal with the lessons they were assigned. Time management became a major priority for them. Naturally, some did better than others.

For their part, Anand and Pranav took to spending any spare time with the students, to gauge their comfort level and check on their learning progress. The brothers were keen to succeed and their hands-on approach seemed the best way.

Anand taught mathematics, and his old students taught the physics and chemistry portions. Pranav Kumar took care of the management aspects of the school.

After the first couple of weeks, when everyone had become more used to each other and the Super 30 programme as well, the days eventually assumed a routine that has varied very little over the years.

A typical day would start with the students assembling in the classroom and going over the previous day's lessons and problems. After eating, the students would assemble in the classroom and go over the previous day's lessons and problems. Anand or one of the instructors would join them, and lessons for the day would begin. Even today, this is how the day begins for Super 30 students.

They were now into the second week of the programme. Anand went in to find the students in groups, discussing some problem or the other. They quietened down and went back to their benches when they realized their teacher had arrived.

From his position at the front of the classroom, Anand could see the faces of all his students. He liked to examine their reactions to understand how well they absorbed what he was teaching. It was warm and he had a towel around his shoulders to wipe away the sweat from his brow. Anand's style of teaching was animated and very expressive. He would gesticulate often and wore the chalk down fast. From the very beginning, he created an environment of challenging methods, asking questions. His oft-repeated line in the classroom was, 'Is there another way to solve this problem?' He taught the students to understand the fundamental nature of the problem and then come up with different ways to arrive at a solution. He'd tell them, 'There's never just one path to get out of problems in life. And so it is with maths.'

To make the lessons more interesting and engaging, Anand used two fictitious characters as part of his methodology. The first was Ricky, an urban boy dressed in jeans and branded clothing, and hailing from an affluent background. The second was Bholu, who was from a rural background, wearing the traditional kurta-pyjama. Ricky was fluent in English while Bholu was more comfortable in Hindi and local dialects of Bihar. Ricky had been educated in a well-known private school while Bholu had gone through the village education system. The students of Super 30 could identify better with Bholu.

So on a multimedia projector, Anand shows that a question appears on the blackboard in front of Bholu and Ricky. Ricky is able to solve the question quickly and starts to mock Bholu who is still working on it. He says, 'See, I have solved it. You government-school kids are too slow. You don't have proper education, no good coaching.'

Bholu looks up and says, 'You think education can be bought? You think it is imparted only in big schools? It is gained through dedication and devotion. See I have solved the question you solved too. But I have solved the same question through algebra, trigonometry, calculus, complex numbers and geometry, and can do it through countless others methods as well.' Bholu then generalizes the question; since he is preparing for IIT, and has a science background. Related to this question, Bholu can create others himself. 'Now, tell me,' Bholu asks Ricky, 'who is the hero, you or me?'

Anand's purpose was to show his students that despite their differences, Bholu was every bit as good as Ricky, and possibly better, when it came to learning and success, because he had only himself to rely on. Where Ricky would turn to expensive books, computers and other electronic gadgetry designed to making learning easier, in all his examples, Bholu and the Super 30 students would use only their brains and rely on each other for help. Anand's goal was to instil confidence in his students by letting them know that in spite of their lack of access to the best schools and computers, or knowledge of English, they could still crack the IIT JEE. He wanted them to dream big, apply themselves, and work hard. He also tried to make them understand that human values and dignity were not predicated upon access to wealth, and that everyone deserved to be treated with respect and to be given opportunities.

What helped Anand really get through to the students was his hallmark quality of making mathematical concepts crystal clear, his problem-solving approach and his attention to detail. He knew he had to devise an effective method of imparting the knowledge they needed to achieve success in the IIT JEE. His style resonated with his students and they were able to understand him and also communicate with him easily.

The teaching would go on for most of the day. After the morning lessons were over, Jayanti Devi, with her helpers, would serve the students lunch, which on most days consisted of rice, chapattis, dal and vegetable curry. Jayanti Devi had thought of everything and designed a hearty lunch to see the students through the rest of their lessons for the day. *'Badiya'* (excellent), was the way the students described the food. Every Super 30 student till today will tell you that the sumptuous meals always left them satisfied. For many, it's a far cry from what they've been used to most of their life. With the meals cooked in a small kitchen adjoining the classroom and the firewood not being seasoned enough on most days, smoke from the wet wood often permeates the schoolroom. However, the cooking vessels and the steel plates and cups are kept sparkling clean, and Jayanti Devi's frail hands do most of the cutting, chopping, cooking and cleaning. The process is repeated twice a day, seven days a week.

For all that she does, students over the years have come to call Jayanti Devi 'ma'. In those early days of 2002, she put in her everything so the students wouldn't be in want of anything. She was as invested in the success of Super 30 as her sons. Now her heart swells with pride when she sees her children do so well. Very rarely does she leave Shanti Kutir, but these students travel far and wide after they leave Super 30 and that is enough for her. Quite often the whole family joins the students while eating, and the scene resembles one of a very large family with Jayanti Devi fussing over all the kids.

The whole complex of the classroom, kitchen and the courtyard is about 600–700 square feet. It is doubtful if any other institution has produced as many IIT JEE successes from such modest surroundings. There is a small pumpkin patch to add to the beauty of the cramped surroundings.

Lunch would be followed by more lessons, but by about 3 p.m. the students were dismissed from the classroom. Most retired to their respective rooms at the nearby hostel where they slept. In the early days, Anand and Pranav had found lodgings nearby, wherever possible, but in time they came to build a hostel that was rudimentary yet fitted with basic amenities for these students. Now, the brick-walled building is multistoreyed, with staircases both narrow and slippery. About fifteen or so students occupy five rooms between them at any given time. Each student has a very basic bed made of wood, covered by a thin cotton sheet. The thickness of the pillows is less than a few inches, and they barely serve to support the heads of the students, whose primary asset is the brain in those heads. For most students, however, such meagre assets are near luxury when compared with where they come from. They are pleased just to have running water and a functioning toilet.

In the late afternoon and into the evening, the students work together to solve the maths and science problems given to them for practice. They can often be found at the back of the classroom, sitting on the ground, going over the homework and trying to arrive at answers to satisfy their demanding teachers the next day. They fill their notebooks with notes and calculations, formulae and jottings. The noises and happenings from the streets nearby can be tempting, but rarely interrupt their train of thought. Somehow they intuitively understand that they have been given a rare opportunity, and few are prepared to mess it up.

None of the students have any access to computers but that doesn't hold them back because computers don't really help them understand what they're trying to learn. Instead, they work together, bounce ideas off one another, and help each other with the material they'll need to achieve success in the IIT JEE tests—it's almost as if they start to live the curriculum.

Over the years, many people have asked Anand, 'What is the secret of Super 30?' To answer, one is tempted to point at this camaraderie which the students share, cooped up as they are with their one goal, being given, for once in their lives, a chance to escape their fate. They think nothing of staying up late to finish an exercise. At some point in the evenings, one of the students will invariably brew a pot of elaichi chai to help fight off the fatigue that routinely sets in late at night. When a question stumps them all, they turn it into a group activity. They argue, reason and interrupt each other until they find an answer that is acceptable to them. To pump blood into their tiring brains, they get up, walk around the partially-walled rooms, occasionally share a joke or two, then hunker down again to apply themselves to the problem they are tackling.

The power of group-learning activities was and always is in full force for Super 30, and it is the group that helps the students to grow personally as well. It only takes a few weeks after the Super 30 programme commences for the normally diffident and shy students to begin showing more assertiveness. Their social interactions improve by leaps and bounds. Their hard work begins to bear fruit. Solving tough questions gets a little easier. Together they begin to blossom like crops on fertile land patches that lie along the shore of the Ganges River. It is common to see frowns of concentration crease their faces as they wrestle with a particularly difficult problem, and then smiles of victory break out when they achieve success. They support each other and cling to one another for mutual benefit. And no matter where they are—in the classroom or back in the hostel—Anand Kumar is there to prod, provoke, encourage, share, soothe, listen, teach, and generally, to be a surrogate father. He is the person they look up to when they're falling behind. He knows their family backgrounds, and the struggles they have encountered to make their way to Super 30. Over the course of the last thirteen years, he has tutored 390 students for Super 30, and it's amazing how well he remembers them all—their names, their circumstances, how they fared during the exams and where they are today.

If he felt their spirits flagging or inertia setting in, Anand would say, 'You have come from poverty, I come from poverty. The inequality may be in our circumstances but there should be no inequality as far as hope and aspirations go. It is up to you to not only heave yourself out of poverty, but also your family, your society. You cannot lose hope.' Invoking Swami Vivekananda, Anand would urge them to, 'Arise! Awake! And stop not until the goal is reached.'

During this time when the students are away, there is little contact with their family. In the early days no one could afford cell phones and even now there will be only one mobile among five to six students, which they use sparingly to call home. It may seem amazing that they stay away from staples like cricket, Bollywood films, and other usual entertainment for youth . . . but as Anand tells them, there will be enough time for all this once they make something of themselves.

Now, there is a certain confidence that if you're accepted to Super 30, and if you study hard and learn all you need to know, there is a very good chance of passing the IIT JEE. Back during the inception phase in 2002–03, however, there was no such confidence. The students were charting untested waters, and the man who led the way was jittery too. But once that everyday routine had been set, focus and success was instilled into the whole exercise, reinforcing the tutors' efforts and hard work, and so Anand stuck to the schedule he had first devised in 2002. Year after year, that compound has seen students come in, settle into the Super 30 programme and pass their exams fighting all kinds of odds. Anand is the constant who brings the same levels of passion, inspiration, and hard work to the crusade.

Winter was slowly slipping away, and Anand found himself up late at nights worrying over the approaching entrance exams. The exams were still a little way off still but Anand felt that he had learned everything he could about the exams and what was needed to pass them. He thought his curriculum was satisfactory but still, he pored over revision papers and thought of ways in which he could prepare the students for what to expect in a few months.

But in the mornings, when he was in class, he felt heartened again. These kids had come a long way since they had first stepped into the classroom. He felt extremely encouraged by their commitment and their response to his challenges. In the run-up to the examination date, he spent more and more one-on-one time tutoring the students and helping them overcome their personal anxieties. Though a selfless teacher, Anand also had a point to prove.

After a year of knitting this elaborate dream and working so hard, the day of the examination finally dawned on them. Across the world, the IIT JEE is one of the most difficult examinations to crack. Only about 10,000 students out of more than 15,00,000 pass the exam, and at his most optimistic, Anand Kumar allowed himself to dream that four or five of his students might make the cut.

The days leading up to the result were nerve-racking. When the result came, Anand almost couldn't believe it. He had been stressing out for so long about this that for a few moments he went completely numb. A few students were with him at that moment, and before he knew it he was being tackled to the ground by these boys. Eighteen students had made it. EIGHTEEN! Anand felt a shiver go down his spine when he saw who had the highest rank. Abhishek Raj. The same boy who had come to Patna with no money in his pocket, mother in tow, promising to pay the fees when the potato harvest came in.

Jayanti Devi beamed and tried to bravely wipe tears from her face. Pranav kept exclaiming, 'I knew it!' All the support staff, neighbours who weren't sure what exactly had happened, everyone, hugged each other and celebrated. It was like India had defeated Pakistan in the Cricket World Cup final. Sixty per cent of the class had cleared the exam—in the first attempt! And the remaining twelve also got into institutes of repute.

What followed was truly unprecedented. No one could have predicted this scale of success for Super 30. This first attempt was like a shot in the arm for Anand and all who had supported his dream. This was just the beginning of a revolution that was stirring in a pocket of Bihar. But it seared and soon it was discovered by the Indian press, by the government, and eventually the international media came knocking—everyone wanted a piece of this magic that Anand Kumar had woven.

StudentSpeak

Name: Shivangee Gupta

Super 30 Batch: 2012–13

Institute and Stream: Chemical Engineering, Indian Institute of Technology Roorkee (IITR)

Current Job: Student

Iam from an underprivileged family family, hailing from a village near Kanpur. My father has a magazine and newspaper stall and we are five people in the family. I finished my secondary education from a government school. I got to know about Super 30 and was fortunate enough to clear the test and started preparing for the IIT JEE in Patna.

Regarding the atmosphere at Super 30, I stayed at sir's home and his family treated me like one of their own family members. We were provided with all coaching in Patna, all free of cost including our stay etc. It was a year full of learning and experiences, and overall a memorable one.

Daily, we had theory classes and then got assignments which were to be completed at home. Anand sir was very motivating in the classes. His mere presence and telling us the success stories of his previous students in the class was a source of morale and inspiration that kept us going.

Regarding his teaching methodologies, he emphasized that we see the problem from different angles and come up with as many ways to solve the same problem. In the theory classes, he gave us examples and solved a single problem using different methods. Similarly, we prepared for chemistry and physics subjects at Super 30 too. In addition to academics, he also taught his students how to be good human beings.

And finally I cleared the IIT JEE. I am currently in my third year studying chemical engineering at IIT Roorkee. I faced initial problems regarding fee expenses for study at IIT. Super 30 helped me with getting a loan from a bank for my studies by giving the guarantee required for the procedure. In addition to that, Anand sir has always been a source of help, inspiration and guidance one way or the other, even after three years of leaving Super 30.

I am very grateful and indebted for all the help, education and inspiration I've received from Anand sir.

6

Origin Tales

By 2013, word about Super 30 had spread far and wide, both nationally and internationally. An eighteen-year-old boy, who lived near the Nepal border, travelled for two nights with the hope of joining the Super 30 class that year. The son of a poor family, he had convinced his ageing parents that he could persuade Anand Kumar to include him in the Super 30 programme. He had scored 90 per cent in maths at school and might have done better had he been able to attend more classes, instead of working in the fields assisting his parents. None of this mattered, however, for it was all water under the bridge. Super 30 would change his fortune, as well as that of his family, and he dreamed of what that life might be like as made his journey by train to Patna.

Although the distance was only a few 100 kilometres, the journey took more than eighteen hours. He had a little over 500 rupees in his pocket, but carried dreams of how the programme would propel him to a successful run at the IIT JEE exams and a good job afterwards, where he could earn a million dollars. Both his dreams and sleep were cut short when the train roared into Patna, its thundering horn waking every sleeping soul in the neighbourhood.

With a small, modest box in his hand, and a bag on his back, the young man made his way to the Ramanujan School with very high expectations. At about 9 a.m. he arrived at the famed school. From a distance he saw the famous teacher, Anand Kumar, on a platform teaching a group of students. The students took notes with the utmost attention. The din of the traffic nearby seemed to disturb none of them.

The boy waited for the break to approach Anand Kumar. The anticipation of meeting the teacher provoked small waves of anxiety, and he found himself sweating, not because it was hot, but because he was nervous. When the break came he was forced to stew a bit more because Anand Kumar was swarmed by a large number of students wanting to clarify doubts. Finally the boy drew courage and pushed his way to the forefront, raising his right arm while simultaneously calling out, 'Anand sir.' Not recognizing the boy, Anand immediately waved him into his crammed office, and then finished with his students before entering the office himself. With kindness, he asked the boy what he wanted, though he had a pretty good idea already.

'Sir, I want to join Super 30. Please help me. I will work hard, I promise you.' It was a common enough request, one Anand Kumar had heard from thousands of boys since the inception of Super 30 a decade ago. He inquired about the youth's background, his exam scores at school, and about his financial status. Finally, Anand paused and looked at the young man with compassion in his eyes.

'I'm afraid you have made the long journey for nothing. Have you not heard about the entrance exams for Super 30? The exams are over for this year and we have filled all the seats.'

Anand could see the devastation in the boy's eyes, but all he could do was to give him details about the next set of entrance exams. Unhappily, the boy left to return to his family, having learned one important lesson—that if you want something in life, you have to approach it from the correct path and work hard for it.

This young man's story is just one of the thousands Anand feels tugging at his heart every day. He knows that it's impossible to help every young person who crosses his threshold, but that doesn't make the experience of turning them away any less painful. He knows that for a great majority of the youth who journey to see him, Super 30 might well be their only hope for getting out of the slums and villages where poverty and prejudice rule.

Anand felt that any lapses on his part would lead to a culture of laxity and disregard for rules, which he wanted to shield Super 30 from. Just because the programme was borne out of kindness, there was no reason why it shouldn't be rigorous. In fact, Anand believed that these sets of rules and effective testing methods that examined a potential student's intellect and ability to withstand the rigour of the IIT JEE exams were imperative to Super 30's success. Every year, hundreds of hopeful young people approach the Super 30 programme in the hope of passing its entrance exams so that they can study with the famed Anand Kumar, and every year hundreds of them are turned away. If it somehow seems unfair then that's another important lesson to be learned—life often isn't fair, but there's always a chance to change one's fortunes if one is prepared to persevere.

Perseverance was the key to success for one young man who joined Super 30 in 2009.

Anup Raaj was different. His life strangely seemed to remind Anand of his own. Anup was from a tiny, impoverished village called Chenw in the foothills of the Aurangabad district, between Bodh Gaya and Nalanda in Bihar.

Anup's father, Rampravesh, was a somewhat educated man who was chronically unemployed when Anup was a young boy, though not from want of trying. His mother, Meena Devi, was a housewife who tended to Anup and Rampravesh's needs to the best of her ability, but there was always a shortage of food supplies, which meant that meals were typically limited to basic chapattis and dal. Rampravesh had tried his hand at business but that had failed too. A future in Chenw offered little hope, and his inability to provide for his family drove Rampravesh nearly insane. On many occasions he was seen muttering to himself while roaming the streets looking for work.

In Bihar, due to the gap in the months between the sowing of crops and harvesting them, there is no work to be found for most people who are dependent on agriculture. Rampravesh was one such person. One rainy evening in August, inside the modest house Anup suddenly started crying.

'What happened, beta?' Anup's mother Meena asked her son worriedly.

'*Ma, khana,*' Anup whimpered.

But there was no food in the house. Feeling helpless, Meena checked the various tins and pans but there was nothing she could feed her son. She sank down to the floor and tears silently started running down her cheeks. Rampravesh couldn't bear to see his wife and son in such a state. 'I'll get some dal and chawal from somewhere; don't worry,' he told them.

'Just get some rice. I will boil it and we can have it with salt,' Meena told her husband.

Rampravesh nodded but thought, where will they find rice? Even the bania moneylender had stopped extending credit . . .

'You prepare the chulha by lighting the firewood and set the water to boil. By then I will be back,' he told Meena and went out of the house.

It took Anup's mother half an hour to prepare and then put the water in the pan. The water started to boil. The firewood burned out, and the water cooled down. But Rampravesh did not return. They grew very worried; added to hunger was fear about his whereabouts.

At first light, Anup's mother decided to go look for her husband herself.

During Anup's childhood, the villages in the Aurangabad district had, and still have, another problem that plagues the people who are just trying to survive. The region, for the past fifty years or so, has been a spawning ground for terrorism and political violence. Grinding poverty, starvation, lack of opportunity, cronyism and corruption have led many in that region to embrace a violent form of Maoism. Calling themselves Naxalites, they regularly kill government officials and policemen, and extort money from wealthier people through abduction. Killing those who betray them is also common.

The Naxalites live amongst the people in the region, though few know who they are. Red cloths mark the sites of their operations, and villagers know they should avoid those areas or risk death. The villagers are aware of these operations but they do not stay to witness the depredations, which makes it difficult to apprehend the Naxalites afterwards. When the red flags disappear, the villagers come out of their homes and life returns to normal. This is one of the key reasons tourists avoid this route to visit Bodh Gaya and the holy shrine of Lord Buddha.

On that day, Meena went to the Naxalite areas and asked them about Rampravesh. But the Naxals said, what will we do with your husband, woman? She visited the local police station and pleaded her case but the officer she spoke with wasn't much help. 'If he is alive, he will return on his own,' was the response she received to her inquiries. Anup and Meena never saw Rampravesh again. The boy had been nine years old.

Until that time, Anup had not attended school. Instead, he'd spent most of his time on farms or running errands for his family. He had acquired a basic understanding of how to sow rice, and he could carry gunny sacks from the farms to the shops to enhance the income of the family. Sleeping under the shade of trees offered some comfort on a hot, sunny day, but most days were about work and trying to find the family's next meal. Books were something he occasionally flipped through to check for pictures, but mostly, they didn't make any sense to him.

His father's disappearance left the boy with many questions, and a big hole in his heart. Days and months passed, and he thought of his father often. Questions remained about his father's disappearance but there were no answers. Meena decided her son needed an education, and she arranged for him to attend the local village school. But the classes were small and sparsely staffed. Students sat on dilapidated floors while classes ran, and the standard of education was like the floors . . . broken and uneven.

On the other hand, even having a group of students and teachers under one roof in the village of Chenw was considered a big success. Such a thing had been unprecedented even a decade earlier. The villagers were ever so grateful to the teachers for their services. They offered grain, vegetables, milk and eggs as gifts. Anup joined the students, and though his performance was just average, he was able to move on to Class VII. It was at this point that Anup decided to take more interest in his schooling. If he was going to have to walk that far to get to school, braving the rain, floods and other disruptions, he grew determined to make it worth the slog. He often thought about his father as he walked the lonely and dusty roads of Chenw each day.

With this determination, he went on to score 84.8 per cent in the Bihar board exams. The marks were excellent by all standards. The whole village was proud. Celebrations lasted for a few days. On this occasion, Meena cried again, but this time for joy. Unfortunately, the celebration was short-lived because harsh reality quickly set in again. Without fatherly guidance or money, a future education was not likely, but Anup and Meena weren't prepared to give up. They managed to scrape together enough money so that he could enrol in Gaya College to complete Class XI. Once again, Anup studied hard and excelled in his exams, scoring 81.8 per cent. However, without informing Meena, he secured a job at a local courier company to alleviate the financial burden on his mother. Meena was very upset when she learned about Anup's decision and dissuaded him from doing so. She coaxed him to concentrate on his education instead.

Anup, like most aspiring students, made appointments to visit various coaching institutions in Patna to inquire about the fees needed to attend those facilities. The sum—Rs 100,000–200,000 for two years— was unaffordable for him. He walked the streets of Patna examining billboards for news of coaching institutes. Some boasted high success in IIT JEE exams, while others boasted about highly qualified teachers. Some exhibited photographs featuring successful students and testimonials. Anup found it difficult to verify any of these claims. Besides, Anup did not have the money anyway. He returned to Chenw to discuss matters with his mother. She urged him not to give up hope.

In Patna, Meena with her son tried to approach the chief minister of Bihar, Nitish Kumar, for help regarding some programme that could prepare Anup for a career in engineering. When they arrived at the chief minister's residence, a helpful official told them that they didn't run any programme of the sort and instead told them about Super 30. He scribbled down a phone number and the address for the Super 30 programme, and gave it to Anup, telling him to contact Anand Kumar. 'If he accepts you in Super 30, your financial and other issues will be solved. He does not charge any money for coaching, food and accommodation.' The words were the most soothing Anup had heard in the past years, and as he left the office he felt content for the first time in a long time.

Shortly after they made contact with Anand Kumar over the phone, an appointment was made and mother and son came to meet Anand.

'How long have you been in Patna?' Anand asked them.

'Since four days, babu,' Meena replied.

'Where are you staying?'

'We don't have any place to stay; all day we look for coaching or some assistance; and at night, exhausted, we spread out a newspaper and sleep at the railway station. We eat some dry chana and murmura and drink water from the taps.'

Anand observed this woman who was barefoot in this blistering heat but saw no signs of bitterness or frustration on her face. Instead, he was amazed by the hope and determination she displayed. She truly believed that her son was intelligent and had the makings of a successful man. *Such is this world; some kids get to study in five-star schools but are more interested in Facebook and partying; and here is another reality.* Anand was very moved.

'Well, the Super 30 test is scheduled five days from now. If you have it in you, you will be through. Here we test a student's aptitude. The questions are basically of an intermediate level, but conceptual type,' Anand told Anup and his mother. Meena pleaded with Anand to let Anup bypass the exam but her pleas fell on deaf ears as Anand insisted he could not bend the rules. Five days later Anup took the test, but failed to make the cut by a whisker. He was devastated.

Anand could not shake off Anup's story from his mind for some reason. He learned more about his background, the loss of his father, the deprivation and the struggle of living under the terror of the Naxalites in Chenw. He also learned about the resilience the youth had shown through his struggles. Showing the compassion that has been a hallmark of his career, Anand Kumar told Anup he thought he had what it took to succeed in the IIT JEE, so decided to bend the rules slightly to help one more gifted but poor young man. The other factor to consider was that he had sat for the exam and only missed the cut-off by the smallest margin.

As for why he permitted himself to bend the rules for this one boy when he wouldn't do so for others, Anand realized that the paths open to a smart, gifted, young man in a place like Chenw were extremely limited. It didn't take much imagination to see that someone like Anup might easily be led into the life of violence that was prevalent around his village. Being smart and ambitious, he could have emerged as a gang lord, or possibly a commander of the

Maoists, and he could have made his money from extortion and murder. He wouldn't have been the first. Anand considered how many other bright young lads had drifted down this treacherous path, and decided that Anup wasn't going to be one of them if he could help it.

As it has turned out, instead of possibly becoming a part of the problem in Chenw and the surrounding region, Anup has become a source of inspiration to the young kids of Chenw. He succeeded admirably in the IIT JEE and went on to study at the Indian Institute of Technology, Mumbai.

In May 2010, Patna was caught up in political strife when national political parties called for a one-day, all-India national strike. Life in Patna would come to a screeching halt that day if the protests went ahead as planned. To their horror, thousands of students who had prepared for the Super 30 entrance test, including Anup and the other students, discovered that the national strike would coincide with the date of the entrance exam.

Sure enough, transportation was not readily available that day, but the students found a way to get to the Bankipore Girls' High School in Patna. Some had to jump over roadblocks, while others had to travel several days in advance to make it to the centre. In addition, there was the fear of being pelted by rocks. The police had imposed curfew on the more violent and sensitive parts of the city to maintain law and order.

Fortunately, common sense prevailed amongst the leaders of the various political parties that were calling for the strike. Knowing the popularity of Super 30 and the importance of the exams, they allowed students free passage because they realized barring the students from taking the exams might cost them dearly in the polls later on. So, while the heart of Patna was deserted because of the strike, hundreds still gathered at the Bankipore Girls School to write the exam. There was no police presence at the examination centre. On that day, Anup and his fellow students triumphed.

The collective learning experiences at Super 30 had a transformational effect on Anup, but not only on him. His success means many students in Chenw are now opting for higher education, and more are saying no to violence as a quick solution to their problems.

Anup Raaj's story is just one of the 390 stories of young, impoverished youth who have made the journey to Shanti Kutir to learn at the feet of Anand Kumar and his fellow teachers. Of the almost 390 students over the past thirteen years, 333 of them have passed the IIT JEE. It's a feat that is unequalled by any other coaching programme in India, and when one considers the backgrounds of the desperate but hopeful students who come each year, it's quite amazing that any of them have managed to succeed.

Another beacon of light is Nidhi Jha. The daughter of an autorickshaw driver, Nidhi was from Varanasi. Sunil Jha had four daughters, one son and one lone dream— that his children should not have to deal with the bottomless poverty that had him driving an auto all his life. But he had no money to afford private education.

Nidhi was admitted into Sanatan Dharam Inter College. Right from the start, she was a dedicated student spending hours poring over her second-hand, frayed textbooks. When she passed her Class X exams, it was as if she had achieved the unthinkable. This gave her confidence to pursue a dream that she had borrowed from many parents who prayed at the nearby temple. She often heard them praying, 'Please make my son a doctor, God. Please make him an engineer.' Without any outside guidance or formal coaching, armed only with old, hand-me-down books, she started preparing for the IIT entrance exam. But she was unsuccessful; she could not clear the exam.

Her dream was shattered. She cried and cursed her luck, and dejected, took admission in a bachelor's of science programme in a government college. Then, one day, in a newspaper, she read about Super 30. Her eyes, which had lost the fire of hope, shone again. She went to Patna and on clearing the test, became a part of Super 30. As there are much fewer girls in Super 30 than boys, she became a part of Anand's family. She called Jayanti Devi 'dadi' and studied diligently with a single-minded focus. The state of the family—her father driving an autorickshaw, her grandfather selling namkeen, her chacha a driver in someone's service, kept revolving in her mind. Only this drove her to study further. At times, Jayanti Devi would tell her to take a little break, maybe watch a little TV to relax, but she said, 'Dadi, I have my whole life to do all these things. I will not get a chance like this again.'

The result came, and Nidhi had made it. She went on to study engineering in the Indian School of Mining (ISM), Dhanbad. Pascal Plisson, a French director, made a film on Nidhi's life. The film was released in 2015; and Nidhi's family, along with Anand and Pranav, went to Paris to watch the premiere. It was an absolutely surreal moment for Nidhi's family who had lived a life of penury in Varanasi and suddenly they were seeing things they could have never dreamed of had it not been for their daughter.

When Anand and Pranav saw posters with Nidhi's photo on the streets of Paris, the two brothers were overcome by gratitude and a sweeping sense of how far these kids had come.

The story of Satyendra Prasad Singh and his family is equally compelling. He is a small-time farmer who invested everything he had a single buffalo so that he could feed his family. He sold buffalo milk in his neighbourhood and to local merchants, but there wasn't much money to be made from the milk business. A small, postage-stamp-sized plot of land was the only other possession that Satyendra Prasad owned besides the buffalo. Grazing the animal and catering to its needs was wearing out and challenging. Flooding from the Ganges ruined their plot of land during the monsoon seasons, so any hope of augmenting the meagre living made from selling buffalo milk was limited.

Needless to say, Satyendra Prasad did not want his son, Alok, to suffer the same fate. Fed up with the recurring failure of his business, he decided to sell his plot of land because of debilitating poverty. The villagers deemed it a suicidal move. He did not reveal his purpose in selling to anyone except his family and close friends. Taking the money, he made his way to Patna to enrol Alok in a better school than the one in the local village. He knew that education in their village was as lifeless as the dried hay that he was feeding his cattle.

Satyendra's plan did not disappoint. By sending Alok to school, Satyendra Prasad grappled with near starvation but had hope that their situation would improve. On completing his schooling, Alok was accepted into Super 30, and later into IIT. Now he is working as an engineer at Power Grid. Today, when Alok returns home for the holidays, the village kids flock to him. The once-abandoned village school is seeing improved attendance. Satyendra Prasad continues to run his buffalo business, but he is much less burdened about the future now that his son is making something of himself.

In many ways, the students who go through the Super 30 experience the same trials and tribulations, joys and elation that any other high-level team endures over time. They work together, live together, laugh and joke together, butt heads, patch things up, share each other's personal lives, and sink or swim together as a team.

Naturally, it doesn't hurt to have a great coach when you're on a team, and Anand Kumar and his family have served as exemplary role models over the years. Goodwill, calm and empathy on the part of the Kumar family have been a solid rock for the students to ground their trust upon. Most students incorporate the qualities of their coach into their daily experience and are all the better for it.

StudentSpeak

Name: Abhishek Raj

Super 30 Batch: 2003 (first ever batch of Super 30)

Institute and Stream: Geophysics, IIT Kharagpur

Current Job: Area Geophysicist, Schlumberger, Moscow

I was born in a remote village of Bihar named Rasalpur. My family was a marginal farming family of Bihar. I completed my schooling and intermediate examinations from Bihar Sharif and then went to Patna to prepare for IIT JEE. I was not conventionally selected for Super 30 by appearing in the Super 30 entrance exams since my rank fell short a bit. I did not have money to join a practice test programme for JEE so I asked Anand sir to give me a chance in his test series. Fortunately, I did very well on the first test and Anand sir asked me to join the team.

It was an entirely different experience while we were all studying together in the team. Anand sir provided everything for us including food, accommodation and classes to improve our concepts. Most of the teachers I have studied with are concept-oriented persons; however, Anand sir is a problem-solving-oriented person. He used to define or develop concepts on the basis of most of the problems under the topic (a unique thing about him). Every week he used to ask us about what we found to be the weakest topic or a difficult chapter and then he used to organize classes to specifically tackle them. Anand sir created an ultimate competitive environment for JEE with just one aim—'Succeed in JEE, succeed in life.' I would like to thank him for providing this kind of opportunity for me and hundreds of students like me. I think he has been motivating millions of students every day by creating this kind of institution.

7

A Brighter Tomorrow

After the unprecedented results of 2003, Anand went about conducting the selection process for a new batch of Super 30 with encouragement and renewed zeal. But with the good press and laudation, a festering problem raised its ugly head again. The coaching industry in Patna was as notorious as it was widespread, and there had been poisonous jealousy brewing for some time now. The reason was almost simple, but not quite. For starters, Anand Kumar was fast emerging as the most competent mathematics teacher in India. Therefore he became the obvious choice for aspiring students seeking coaching in the subject. Anand was no stranger to such negative propaganda and responded to it through a reinforced commitment to further education.

Things became heated though when criminals too entered the fray, especially a dreaded gangster who was serving a life sentence in the local high-security jail. His name is famous for all the wrong reasons. Criminals of all shades of evil in Bihar had learned to avoid confrontation with this rogue. Allegedly, even behind bars, this gangster had great clout. Extortion was easy for him.

One day in 2003, Anand and Pranav were talking to a cousin, Vivek Singh, who was visiting. The landline rang and their cousin picked up the phone.

'Hello?'

'Give the phone to that master. Tell him his worst nightmare is calling.'

'Who is this?'

'You don't know who I am?' The gangster went on to give his name. 'Give the phone to that master now.'

Anand was worried. Why would such a person call him? Pranav took the receiver from Vivek and asked, 'Yes, what do you want?' but the line had been cut by then.

The phone rang again. This time Anand picked up. The gangster started threatening Anand and abusing him.

'I know who you are. You are that kid who couldn't make it through the Super 30 test, right? Why are you threatening me by pretending to be someone else? You should be ashamed. I will report you to the police,' said Anand and slammed the phone down.

Then the phone rang again.

'Abey o master, you don't recognize me? I will ruin your life.'

Anand tried to admonish him but Pranav took the phone. The gangster went on to rain abuses on him and said, 'Tell this

Anand Kumar to stop pretending to be some messiah and helping the poor. Tell him I will have him killed if he doesn't shut down his institute. Do your coaching and pass on some riches to us. But stop trying to be a mahatma.' It was clear that the caller was indeed the gangster. Anand was at a loss; he was scared and nervous.

Pranav had his wits about him. Seeing Anand waiver, he gave him courage: 'Bhaiya, don't worry. We won't stop Super 30. We'll see what happens. Let's report this to the police. We cannot cower down before such scum.'

Some four or five years later, when the IGP was being transferred from Patna to Delhi, he confided in Anand that this gangster was threatening him because he had been paid by a local politician and some big bureaucrats who were worried by Anand's meteoric rise.

The fear came to roost when an attempt was made to attack Anand just outside his home in 2003. Munna, one of his staff members, stood in the way of the attacker. Munna was stabbed several times in the abdomen but he managed to prevent the attacker from entering the house. Hearing Munna's piercing shouts, the students immediately poured out of the classrooms to the rescue. More than fifty people—from Super 30 and some neighbours—went to the local hospital with Munna, who bled profusely through the journey. When the attending doctors told Anand that they needed blood donors to save Munna, several students raised their hands and eagerly came forward to donate. The students refused to budge till Munna was out of danger. Munna himself believes that it was the prayers of the students and the goodwill of Anand Kumar that saved his life. The scar on Munna's abdomen is a chilling reminder of the dangers that Anand Kumar faces on a daily basis.

Anand was provided with constant protection by two armed police personnel of the Bihar Police who accompanied him thereafter. This decision was taken by the DGP, Bihar. Any harm to Anand Kumar would have posed a serious question mark on the law-and-order situation in Bihar, a state already notorious for its high crime rate. But the protection was soon withdrawn. Then in 2005, when Nitish Kumar's government came into power, this protection was made permanent and with these security arrangements the personal threats have all but stopped.

The next year, in 2004, the number of students who cleared the IIT JEE rose from eighteen to twenty-two. In 2005, the number rose still higher to twenty-six. In 2006, and then again in 2007, twenty-eight students got through this highly competitive test. People started talking. Everyone wanted this 'formula' that Anand Kumar had, his magic touch. But

Anand alone knew what it took. And it was too simple to impress people who expected quick, easy shortcuts. It would shock people when Anand insisted that it was nothing but his belief in his students and the monumental amounts of hard work they put in day and night to prove that their circumstances could no longer hold them back.

Japan has taken great notice of Super 30 over the years, as early as 2005 when the Japanese channel NHK made the first documentary on the school. This was followed by a visit from Japanese actress and former Miss Japan, Norika Fujiwara, to shoot another documentary on Super 30 in 2007. It was really the presence of Miss Fujiwara, who was deeply impressed by Anand Kumar's efforts in Patna, which truly alerted the Indian media to the sensation Super 30 is.

In 2015, two students were selected by the University of Tokyo for higher education with full scholarship. Over the years, Super 30 has been part of several Japanese documentaries and even a book "Indo No Shougeki", published by Japan's famous publisher 'Bhushan' and written by journalists of TV Channel NHK. Japan has lauded the mathematician's vision and championed the cause of Super 30 since before it became famous.

Then came the year of deliverance. By now the Indian media was well onto Anand. They knew this man achieved something extraordinary every year and they would call him often, stay in touch with him and closely follow the waves that he made wherever he went. It was in 2008 that all thirty students cracked the IIT JEE for the first time. It seemed too good to be true. But the feat was repeated in 2009 when Super 30 achieved a cent per cent result again. In the same year the Discovery Channel made a documentary on Super 30, produced by Veronica Hall and directed by Christopher Mitchell. 2010 proved to be a hat-trick year with Super 30 managing the incredible—all thirty students had cleared the exam for the third consecutive year.

In 2010, Barack Obama's special envoy, Rashad Hussain, visited Super 30 and termed it the best institute in the country.

'Super 30 is the best institute in India and an example of change, a dream which US President Barack Obama harbours in the field of education, irrespective of caste and creed,' the US President's special envoy to the Organization of the Islamic Conference said.[1]

Appreciation and recognition flowed thick and fast after that. As more and more people learned about Anand's efforts and successes, encouragement in the form of media attention and special mentions in the media increased. *Time* magazine lauded Super 30 as the Best School of Asia in 2010. *Newsweek* listed it as one of the four most innovative schools in the world. Later, French director Pascal Plisson made the film *The Big Day*, which includes the story of Nidhi Jha who cracked the JEE (advanced) in 2014 and is now studying at ISM, Dhanbad. Closer home, Prakash Jha consulted Anand Kumar when he was making *Aarakshan* (2011), a film which revolves around education and caste-based reservation in the system, starring Amitabh Bachchan, Saif Ali Khan, and Deepika Padukone. Bachchan plays the role of Prabhakar Anand, a principal who in a different arc of the story teaches mathematics to underprivileged students. Amitabh Bachchan acknowledged that this was in part based on Anand Kumar. 'I had to direct Big B and Saif on how their characters should go about teaching mathematics to underprivileged children. And I did not know how to do that. So I requested Anandji to spare some time for me, to which he readily agreed,' Jha said. 'His unique style made our task easy. I am thankful to him for helping me out,' Jha added.[2] Anand went to Jha's office with recordings of simulated classes which were helpful for Amitabh Bachchan and Saif Ali Khan to understand their roles better. It just goes to show the authority Anand has come to enjoy as an exemplary teacher and role model who can relate to not only the students whom he teaches but act as a guide to just about anybody.

Such a turn of events for somebody who rose from very humble beginnings may seem extraordinary, but there were thorns attached to this flowering enterprise.

In 2010, Tarun Gogoi, the chief minister of Assam, visited Super 30 and was very impressed by what he saw there. Interestingly, following his visit, a distress call was made in the name of Super 30 for financial help. Unfortunately the chief minister's office failed to cross-check with Anand Kumar if the call for help was genuine and the crook was able to fleece a substantial amount from the chief minister under the pretext of enrolling in Super 30. This wasn't the first time that attempts had been made to exhort money from people who sympathize with Super 30's cause. Anand has tried to make clear time and again that such pleas should be checked since Super 30 does not run on donations of any kind but on the money earned by the Ramanujan School of Mathematics.

They say that imitation is the greatest form of flattery. It would be wonderful indeed if there were many more Anand Kumars and they could also provide what Super 30 has striven to achieve for over a decade. But so far, this has not been the case and an institution of a similar structure—offering free education, boarding and meals—has not yet come up anywhere else in Bihar. Unfortunately, in an industry as lucrative as the coaching business, it is too easy to try sly methods to dupe unsuspecting students and parents. As the fame of Super 30 grew, many coaching centres mushroomed in and around Patna to cash in on the popularity. Institutions claiming to be Super 50, Super 100 and Super 20 appeared overnight on billboards in the neighbourhood. They tried to confuse people into believing that these were branches of Super 30 or extensions. Some boasted of giving better tuitions, but nobody offered free in-house training. None could match the standards set by Anand Kumar either. As a result, many of them did not last very long and simply sank without a trace.

On his own web page Anand Kumar makes it abundantly clear that there is only one Super 30 in Patna, which is run by him at Shanti Kutir. The same page also clarifies that Super 30 does not seek or accept donations from public undertakings for the management of the institution.

Another thing that saddens Anand is when people assume that Super 30 selects students on the basis of caste as that makes it easier for students to get admission through reserved quotas. It is untrue and the only factor which is considered is financial backwardness.

Anand is invited to give a talk or a lecture by universities, corporates, government units, on almost a weekly basis. He tries to go as often as he can without compromising on his teaching. He realizes that he is the face of Super 30 and how important it is to make people aware that education is the only answer to unemployment, to unchecked crime in states like Bihar, to caste prejudices, and to poverty which breeds uncountable problems for the country.

Even in the early days, when Anand would pedal past poor students returning home weighed down by gigantic backpacks, he could see stark differences between them and their AC-bus-riding affluent counterparts. He sees how these differences between children of different strata keep increasing without any hope of ever narrowing down, leading to the widening economic gap in India. An obvious solution is that equal opportunity via education will lessen the gap. In 2010, the Right to Education (RTE) came into force, which stipulates free and compulsory education for children between six and fourteen in India under Article 21A of the Indian Constitution. Ideally, this act should ensure that all children are provided with adequate learning during their early years which equips them for higher education. Many incentives like the 'Mid-Day Meal' are also introduced to ensure attendance. According to the Annual Status of Education Report (ASER) in 2014, the enrolment rates of students were near universal at 96.7 per cent.

But the worry is the quality of education and the state of primary schools in rural India. In 2015, the Allahabad court directed that government officials must send their children to government schools to know what the provisions were like, and in turn ensure that better standards prevail.

The court observed that primary schools, which are catering to the needs of 90 per cent of the state's school-going children, were in poor conditions but concerned officials did not care about them.[3]

According to ASER, despite 96.7 per cent enrolment, fewer than one out of every two children in Class V can read a Class II text— up marginally from 47 per cent in 2013. Basic arithmetic skills have actually declined— only 44.1 per cent of Class VIII students could solve division problems, typically part of the curricula in lower standards in most states, down from 46 per cent in 2013.[4]

✎

It's not news that the success or failure of any organization is intrinsically tied to the people involved, and Super 30 is no different. From day one, the staff at all levels has exuded common basic qualities which have contributed to the programme's success, including total dedication to the organization, punctuality, honesty and significant flexibility in their hours of work.

Together, the Super 30 team must surely rank as one of the most successful teaching units in all of India (and possibly elsewhere) when it comes to getting results. The attrition rate is low and the success rate is high. Students who join Super 30 tend to achieve what they want, and while their own hard work and dedication has to be factored into the equation, a good deal of the credit must surely go the family and team led by Anand Kumar, Pranav Kumar and Jayanti Devi. That's because their commitment to their students is unparalleled. From the day those students are accepted into the programme they are the priority. They receive much of the energy and time their instructors and mentors have available each day, and that dedication continues even after the students leave the programme. None of his students ever stray far from his mind, and even those who do not pass the IIT JEE know they can always look to their teacher for advice and support.

For those who do pass the IIT JEE, Super 30's support doesn't end there. Given that all of the students must be in dire straits financially to be accepted in the first place, it only stands to reason that those who are successful will likely face significant challenges paying their way through four years of higher education—tuition, boarding, food and other expenses—at the Indian Institutes of Technology. Anand Kumar is fully aware of the financial demands on these students once they clear the IIT JEE exams, so he has worked on growing his network of contacts in order to help promising students get the funds they need.

In the early years his students faced big obstacles in securing loans from the banks because of their destitute backgrounds. The IIT fees, especially with the recent revision, is a staggering sum for someone whose family struggles to put one square meal a day on the table. And even when the banks were willing to loan the money, a successful candidate still had to come up with a counselling fee of forty thousand rupees before classes began. Loans for the tuition fees might be available, but the initial counselling fees weren't because the students were not yet enrolled. In the past, those students who couldn't afford to pay the costs of their education sought the assistance of moneylenders who were more than willing to charge high interest rates to desperate students.

Anand saw the trap facing students who had been successful at Super 30, but who were facing huge debts at the hands of unscrupulous lenders if they were to continue their studies. Something had to be done, and it wasn't long after Super 30 began that he started exploring avenues to assist his students once they'd cleared the IIT JEE.

Manish Pratap Singh is a very close friend of the Kumar brothers. He also happens to be the branch manager of the Union Bank of India in Ranchi, Jharkhand, and he has long been aware of the difficulties these impoverished students face to complete four years of education at IIT. He gave an idea that Anand should approach banks and establish relationships so that they become flexible in extending loans to Super 30 students, especially for counselling. When a student would go to a bank for an education loan, they would ask for proof of admission. But these kids are trying to get a loan for counselling which comes before admission into the institute. And this situation was very difficult for the banks to understand. In March 2015, Anand even met Union minister of state for finance, Jayant Sinha to request the inclusion of the counselling fee as a part of the loan,[5] and the minister was very forthcoming in his ideas to make bank loans more flexible for such students.

In 2015, the stories of the two brothers, Raju and Brijesh, who had cleared IIT but could not afford counselling fees was picked up by the media. Politicians like Akhilesh

Yadav, Smriti Irani and Rahul Gandhi responded to their need and their fee was waived off.[6] Now banks like IDBI, United Bank, Union Bank of India and others provide loans for the counselling fee, thus removing the financial obstacles that lay in their way.

As important as money is to his students, it's of very little consequence to Anand himself. There have been plenty of opportunities to enrich himself over the years. Well-wishers who want his project to succeed have offered large sums of money to help provide stability or to create opportunities for expansion. Needless to say, opportunists who want to be associated with the Super 30 brand have been buzzing around the programme since the first graduating class achieved so much success.

Anand's unwillingness to let money become a motivator or determining factor in the success or failure of Super 30 and its students has not been lost on friends, including one Rajnish Kumar, who was a student of Anand's in the Ramanujan School. Though Rajnish has followed a different path, having studied economics and law to finally become a legal manager at the Aegon Life Insurance Company based in Mumbai, he has followed the exploits of his friend with interest and appreciation through the years. He's also provided support by offering legal advice to Anand and Super 30 when required. It's fair to say that Rajnish has had plenty of success, but he still admires his friend's unwillingness to bend his principles for the almighty paisa.

He's not changed at all through the years, says Rajnish, pointing out that Anand eats the same food as his students, lives in the same neighbourhood, and engages in most of the same day-to-day activities. Even Anand's clothes are comparable to those his students wear to prove that there are no distinctions between them. Rajnish confirms that from his perspective, Anand's motivation has never been about the money, and that his integrity on this matter 'has been unquestionable'.

'Millions could have been made with his name and fame, but he chooses to be a true teacher; luckily he is the best.'

There's no secret that Anand Kumar attributes these successes to perseverance and the will to succeed. Time after time, whether speaking to his students or to government ministers and business leaders, he has stated his belief that the will to overcome difficulties is the key to success, and that the willingness to persevere even in the face of seemingly insurmountable odds is usually the difference between ultimate success or failure.

'It is the willpower within you that serves as the propellant to success,' is a favourite line for Anand Kumar, one he has used during motivational speeches at the University of Tokyo, British Columbia University, MIT, Harvard, Stanford, IIMs, corporates and even in smaller places such as villages and mohallas.

Anand is often asked by well-meaning parents and other stakeholders why coaching is so indispensable to cracking competitive exams: 'Can't children study on their own?', 'What is the point of higher secondary education if it doesn't prepare one for competitive exams like the IIT JEE?' These are the questions that are often put forth. This culture of going to school in the mornings and then going to tuition classes to study the same syllabi points at the fact that our education system is flawed and in need of complete overhauling. The questions that are asked at the JEE entrance exam are at a completely different level from those for +2. This gap is the key point that needs to be addressed. The JEE format is unique and it is irrational to expect students to tackle it on their own without any guidance, when all they are coached for in schools are how to solve problems in the state/central board papers.

Another limitation at the moment for IIT aspirants is that a student can attempt the JEE Advanced only twice in consecutive years. This poses a serious handicap for the underprivileged students who come from Hindi-medium schools. It takes them longer to familiarize themselves with the methodology of questions, and it often takes them two attempts to get comfortable and actually concentrate on the problem-solving and critical thinking sections.

Anand has been in talks with the government recently to devise a programme where online support can be given to school students who have dreams to become engineers. This way, they will not completely have to depend on expensive private coaching, which is a financial burden on the children and their families.

Over the years, when each new batch of students enters IITs and other institutes, they inundate Anand with a barrage of calls. A common complaint of Super 30 students is that IIT is not what they had imagined or expected it to be. It is possible that other non-Super 30 entrants feel similarly. Imagine the expectations they would have when their every waking moment and some even while asleep has been spent towards trying to get into this esteemed institution. The amount of hard work they put in and what their expectations of such a coveted place would be often don't match up to the reality of the situation.

Anand, over the years, has also learned the ways of the IITs. Many students have complained to him that no one is interested in learning and everyone is caught up in the race to grab the most attractive package at graduation. Even newspapers laud the big packages bagged during placement season. Why are research projects and innovations not given coverage, one wonders. Is it any surprise then that even after being the premier institute in a country of a billion dreams, we are still producing more Satya Nadellas than Mark Zuckerbergs?

A culture of innovation and creativity needs to be encouraged from the very beginning. It is unfair to expect students to suddenly change their outlook to learning when all their lives they are taught to excel by rote learning. The current system does not encourage problem-solving skills, different methods of comprehension and emphasis on the basics. Students spend most of their time memorizing large parts of textbooks and theories rather than imbibing these through targeted learning activities and games. Creativity wrestles with textbook knowledge in a world where test scores decide a student's future, rather than other equally important factors like vision, understanding and potential.

Cambridge, Harvard and MIT are great universities because they have provided the world with solutions and original thought. Anand realizes we are still a little way off when it comes to competing with the best, and this is because students in the system are not taught to question the 'hows' and 'whys' of problems. While teaching at the Ramanujan School and coaching Super 30 batches, Anand tries to instil in his students the habit to question the logic of each solution and also attempt alternative solutions. Anand's style of teaching is a living endorsement of the need for special teachers in the system who can hone an analytical rather than an accepting mindset from the beginning. There is ample research which points at how all children are born intuitive and innovative but set structures and syllabi more often than not stifle this originality.

The same goes for research as well. Anand's early interest in mathematical theory propelled him to conduct research himself and seek out teachers who could help him grow, but he recognizes that if this impetus had been given at the schooling level itself, things might have been easier for him. Even today, the few research projects that do come to the fore are mostly being conducted at the university level by master's, doctorate and post-doctorate students. Taking steps earlier to inculcate the spirit of research would ensure that more and more students foray into this field, leading to a growth in thought leadership and innovation all around.

India has the largest number of people under the age of thirty as compared to anywhere in the world and this statistic suggests one important thing—youth, and therefore potential. It's this same potential that Anand concentrates on when he picks his students for Super 30, and which drives him to provide education to as many people as possible through the Ramanujan School of Mathematics. While India has large human resources, it also has some of the highest number of students competing for seats in premier institutions, i.e., a low level of opportunity for the average individual. Society, the government, and especially you need to get together so that there many more teachers like Anand Kumar can blossom to attempt to eradicate the problems that plague our education system.

Though his audience in recent years is much larger than the small classroom he usually inhabits in Shanti Kutir, his appetite for teaching has not diminished one bit after two decades of tireless efforts. Despite his travels around the world, there's nothing he prefers more than to be with his students at Super 30 and the Ramanujan School where he is most productive. Writing mathematical theorems on the blackboard and challenging his students to find answers is what he enjoys most. His eyes brighten with joy when these young minds develop their own solutions, and that is the greatest satisfaction he can think of, short of the satisfaction he gets from his family.

It was early morning in December 2015, and Anand was standing just outside Shanti Kutir, sorting his thoughts just before another day of bustle began. He was staring into the horizon, mentally planning the day's lessons when his mobile rang. Anand looked at his phone and frowned. It was an unknown number. Anand gave out his number indiscreetly and got several unsolicited calls in a day, from journalists to people inquiring about admissions, to organizers inviting him for guest lectures.

Anand answered the phone. It was a call from a journalist to inquire about the recent honour conferred upon him by the German government. He had been invited to the German state of Saxony where he was honoured by Eva-Maria Stange, minister of state for higher education and research, for his commendable work. He commented on the honour in a few words, put his phone back in his front pocket, and closed his eyes. Behind him, he could hear the rest of the household slowly waking up. He knew any moment his son Jagat would wrestle away from his mother Ritu and come looking for him.

Anand married Ritu, a graduate from IIT Varanasi, in 2008. Ritu was working as a software engineer but since marrying Anand she has devoted herself completely to Super 30 and the plans for its expansion. In 2010, a son was born to them and soon transformed Shanti Kutir and the classroom in a way only a toddler can. Not only was Jagat Kumar the world to Jayanti Devi and the rest of the family, the students of Super 30 would also invariably unwind by playing with the kid.

Anand was startled when he heard someone call his name. Tea was ready. Anand had been reflecting on the future of Super 30 and the so-called fame he now enjoyed, when he saw Munna beckoning to him. In his pensive mood, Anand was reminded of all the challenges they had faced over the years and how Super 30 would be nothing if not for the support he had got from people like Pranav, Ritu, Jayanti Devi, and not least of them—Munna.

As Anand walked into the humble house that has seen such transformative events, he thought fondly of Rajendra Prasad and the great things his father had expected from him. He thought of the great expectations which ride on him. Everywhere Anand goes, youths in great number, in thousands, come out to hear him; to be a part of the revolution in education. Some people think that Anand is a big personality and often some poor woman would come to Anand begging him to teach her nine-year-old son. There have also been cases when a woman whose family was harassing her for dowry turned to Anand for help. Almost every day, no less than ten people come to Anand with requests of varying natures—someone's husband hits them, someone wants their children to be educated, someone has been wrongfully convicted of a crime. They all think Anand can help them. And Anand tries to in some cases, but he also feels ashamed that he cannot do more. In fact, he is helpless. He is only a poor teacher who has no real power. And their beseeching looks, the hope that they pin on him weigh him down. He realizes that Super 30 is only a small beginning. He needs to do a lot more for his country and the poor, to one day become worthy of his father's coat that still hangs on the hanger.

StudentSpeak

Name: Anup Raaj (Anup Kumar)

Super 30 Batch: 2010

Institute and Stream: B. Tech, Civil Engineering, IIT Bombay

Current Job: Co-founder and CTO of PSTakeCare

After getting through Super 30, I was interviewed early and given a spot in the hostel. I cannot forget that place for my entire life. It was a perfect place to study; I don't think any school can provide the same environment, IITs included—white-tiled floors, later we made them blue with our excessive use of blue markers.

That was an inflection point in life. Although I was state rank 11 in Bihar, I had no idea where my life will go. Super 30 became the lifeline. From that moment on, I have never looked back. Let's see where it will all go.

All students had their own strengths and weaknesses. We helped each other to cross the JEE line. Anand sir used to fill us with his immense energy. We used to convert it into a fourteen-hour straight study routine. That practice changed my life. It made me a reader. Now I finish three to four books per month but now the context is business. The matchless 'Ricky and Bholu' story made me realize that I can do it, I can pass the exam. Now it inspires me to think I can do anything, irrespective of my background. Now I am fortunate to have Anand sir as my mentor, friend and guardian. It cannot be explained in writing.

I'll end with the life lessons I learned at Super 30: 'Even in difficult times, you must learn to trust yourself.'

Notes

1. 'Obama's Special Envoy Hails Super 30'. 9 August 2010. *The Hindu*. http://www.thehindu.com/news/national/other-states/obamas-special-envoy-hails-super-30/article559325.ece.
2. Mishra, Alok K.N. 'Big B Gets Teaching Tips from Super 30's Anand'. 31 July 2011.*Times of India*. http://timesofindia.indiatimes.com/india/Big-B-gets-teaching-tips-from-Super-30s-Anand/articleshow/9433908.cms?referral=PM.

3. Sarin, Jitendra. 'Government Staff, Politicos Must Send Their Kids to Govt. Schools: Allahabad HC'. 19 August 2015. *Hindustan Times*. http://www.hindustantimes.com/india/govt-staff-politicos-must-send-kids-to-govt-schools-allahabad-hc/story-COWyikj8YXWbc0CQILw1bO.html.

4. 'Grade F'. 15 January 2015. *Indian Express*. http://indianexpress.com/article/opinion/editorials/grade-f/.

5. Verma, Sanjeev Kumar. 'Plea to Include IIT Counselling Fee in Loan'. 11 March 2015. *Telegraph*. http://www.telegraphindia.com/1150311/jsp/bihar/story_7896.jsp.

6. 'UP Daily Wager Is Happy Father as His Son Cracks IIT'. 21 June 2015. *Hindustan Times*.http://www.hindustantimes.com/india/up-daily-wager-is-happy-father-as-his-sons-crack-iit-govt-waives-fee/story-mAQIE57E1Fs3MSri1XWcWK.html.